Combating Fraud and Corruption in the Public Sector

Combating Fraud and Corruption in the Public Sector

Peter Jones
BSc (Econ), IPFA, MIIA, ACI Arb.

CHAPMAN & HALL
University and Professional Division
London · Glasgow · New York · Tokyo · Melbourne · Madras

Published by Chapman & Hall, 2–6 Boundary Row, London SE1 8HN

Chapman & Hall, 2–6 Boundary Row, London SE1 8HN, UK

Blackie Academic & Professional, Wester Cleddens Road, Bishopbriggs, Glasgow G64 2NZ, UK

Chapman & Hall Inc., 29 West 35th Street, New York, NY10001, USA

Chapman & Hall Japan, Thomson Publishing Japan, Hirakawacho Nemoto Building, 6F, 1–7–11 Hirakawa-cho, Chiyoda-ku, Tokyo 102, Japan

Chapman & Hall Australia, Thomas Nelson Australia, 102 Dodds Street, South Melbourne, Victoria 3205, Australia

Chapman & Hall India, R. Seshadri, 32 Second Main Road, CIT East, Madras 600 035, India

First edition 1993

© 1993 Peter Jones

Typeset by Expo Holdings Sdn Bhd, Malaysia
Printed in Great Britain by Clays, St Ives plc

ISBN 0 412 46370 9

A catalogue record for this book is available from the British Library

Library of Congress Cataloging-in-Publication data
Jones, P. (Peter), 1953-
    Combating fraud and corruption in the public sector/Peter Jones.
— 1st ed.
        p. cm.
    Includes bibliographical references and index.
    ISBN 0-412-46370-9 (alk. paper)
    1. Finance, Public—Great Britain—Auditing.   2 Administrative agencies—Great Britain—auditing.   I. Title.
HJ9925.G7J64   1993
354.410072'32—dc20
                                                          92-27256
                                                          CIP

♾ Printed on permanent acid-free text paper, manufactured in accordance with the proposed ANSI/NISO Z 39.48-199X and ANSI Z 39.48-1984

Contents

Foreword

Why do we have auditors? Peter Jones is to be congratulated for addressing this elusive question in his very readable book.

A question for the experts, many experts will reply. Maybe, but no service provider ever gets the last word about what sort of service is to be provided. Even mediaeval bishops found out the hard way that they could not altogether ignore public opinion. Defenestration was a popular remedy during the Thirty Years War for bishops who failed to respond. Brain surgeons, police chiefs and flight controllers have all had to defer to the market. How can auditors expect to buck this trend?

One factor which has so far given them a bit of undeserved privacy to order their own priorities is that people of good taste never want to put into words what auditors are for. This is obvious from the euphemisms so often used by their technical literature. This often says 'ensure that' when it means 'see if', conjuring up the scenario that everything is really all right, but that auditees just need the auditor to say so. Needless to say no auditor worth the name proceeds on this assumption. The truth needs stating, however, and it is that the public is willing to pay for auditors only if they are looking for something which the public thinks may be wrong.

In the long run discussing professional objectives is the only way for professionals to retain credibility with society. Too many people for comfort are now questioning whether auditors are succeeding. Ministers for their part lose no opportunity to press auditors to widen their repertoires. The sceptics have coined their own word for their doubts – the expectation gap.

Most members of the public would be astounded to hear auditors saying that preventing fraud and corruption are the responsibility of management. Managers are by definition responsible for almost everything which happens on their manors, but it is precisely because managers are responsible for fraud prevention that they feel the need for a regular audit.

I am therefore delighted that Peter Jones has tried to spell out what auditors can do to detect fraud and corruption. It is harder to find books which tell you how to do fraud auditing than how to tickle trout. Some auditors are sure to disagree with the techniques and tests which he describes, but he need not be too put out about this. If the critics can suggest something better, great. A necessary debate will have been opened up.

Will Werry
Chairman of the Competition Joint Committee, freelance
consultant and former district auditor.

Preface

This book explores the circumstances and implications surrounding fraud and corruption in the public sector. In the public sector corporate objectives and regulations are immensely varied and can change frequently, depending upon political initiatives. Public sector bodies are responsible to politicians and, in a democracy, to the electorate. At one extreme organizations may be required to attain a precise level of statutory 'profit' or return on capital employed, while at the other they may be directly funded from taxation with, apparently, little regard for performance.

An underlying theme of this work is the special position and additional responsibilities of public officials who must be seen to be above suspicion of fraud and corruption. The public sector accounts for approximately 40% of the nation's gross national product and financial malpractice can have very serious implications, directly and indirectly, for all its citizens. Two crucial roles are considered, those of auditors and those of managers. When it comes to combating fraud and corruption managers often rely on the assistance and advice of auditors, though the responsibility to prevent malpractice nearly always rests with management. This book attempts to set out some of the objectives and the necessary measures that are, usually, common to both parties and to clarify some of the confusion that can arise. It examines a wide range of financial and organizational wrongdoing and provides detailed case studies which, without intending any comparison with people or organizations current or past, attempt to introduce an element of realism into the explanation of events.

Although investigation and reporting aspects are considered in detail, the book is aimed more at prevention than cure. A great many simple and cost-effective measures can be taken to minimize the risk of fraud and corruption. In a regularly audited and well-managed organization a number of these measures are already likely to be in place. But all too often the underlying significance of such measures is not appreciated by managers, or even auditors. This lack of appreciation can be damaging, particularly during periods of change or when simplistic 'cost-cutting' exercises are undertaken.

Since 1980 all public sector activities have faced increased financial pressures. There have been many different responses often resulting in traumatic organizational changes. After virtually uninterrupted growth for most of the past century, involving an ever expanding controlling and providing role, the public sector now faces contraction and reversion to a more regulatory and enabling role.

It is not the intention of this book to adopt a political stance. The problems of fraud and corruption are more likely than most to be readily transferrable across political boundaries. But any period of fundamental change and realignment offers additional temptations and risks. The detailed effects of change are often unpredicted by their, usually ardent, supporters. Attempts to introduce a more business-like environment with greater competition requires careful forethought. Activities which cause little concern in the private sector will raise many problems if the public sector is allowed merely to 'ape' such activities.

As Chapter 2 explains, historically, many public sector bodies arose to satisfy a demand for goods and services that had not been adequately provided by the market mechanism. Defence is the most obvious example: mercenaries are notoriously fickle. Among important issues involving organizational changes is that of maintaining a strong separation of duties between the public sector client and its contractors which, though always important, was more academic in the past. Today with more and more competitive contracts being awarded, maintaining this separation is a crucial factor in avoiding corruption. Unlike a private entrepreneur a public official should never be able to award valuable contracts on the basis, say, of family or workplace connections. The official must be seen to be above suspicion of favour, even when an arm of the official's own organization is one of the contractors.

Many of the topics covered have been approached from the standpoint of auditors, accountants and financial managers. These professions, particularly auditors, have in recent years been forced to confront the problems caused by fraud and corruption. After several decades of appearing to hope the issue would fade from prominence, the professional bodies, particularly the accounting professions, have started to issue new professional guidance and Parliament has been forced to consider the role of auditors. From occupying a prominent though rarely pre-eminent position until the late 1960s and early 1970s, the influence of fraud and corruption upon the objectives of auditors, both internal and external, has steadily decreased. This has been particularly true of external auditors whose objectives have required them to express increasingly less challengeable opinions over this period. The dramatic reversal of this trend in the 1990s has brought the auditors' role in relation to fraud back to the forefront of debate.

Until the 1948 Companies Act, the external audit of companies required the auditor to attest to the 'truth and correctness' of accounts rather than the current 'true and fair' view. Though impossible actually to fulfil, it was the duty of the National Audit Office to attest to the 'correctness' of accounts until as recently as 1985! But long before this it became accepted by auditors and their clients that, in the main, responsibility for preventing and detecting fraud, lay with management rather than auditors. Well-publicized events in the public and private sectors involving recent fraud and widespread corruption have called into question the independence of auditors and the steps they should take to guard against and report cases of fraud.

The internal auditor, who is generally expected to be of service to management as well as maintaining an independent stance – a position of some invidiousness at times – has tended to be more involved in preventing, detecting and even investigating fraud and corruption than his external counterpart, though the internal auditor in no way compensates for management's own responsibilities.

Throughout this book the examples and case studies are an essential part of understanding the issues and techniques outlined in the main text. Audit, like management, is primarily a vocational rather than theoretical subject, which can be understood and appreciated best by practice and experience. Readers who are unfamiliar with public sector accounting terms may find the appendices of Chapter 9 helpful.

If the techniques and controls discussed in this book are implemented auditors and managers can hope to keep the destructive experiences of fraud and corruption to a minimum for themselves, their colleagues and clients.

Acknowledgements

My wife Pam, my family, close friends and colleagues deserve my grateful thanks for putting up with my inconsiderate behaviour and general rattiness while writing this book.

Various practising auditors, managers and policemen have been kind enough to give helpful advice and opinions, especially on the case studies.

Maxine Moores produced a professionally typed manuscript from a load of scribbled pages and last-minute amendments.

I am also very thankful for my publisher's advice, particularly from Alan Nelson and Steven Reed.

Peter Jones
Faversham

1

Characteristics of fraud and corruption

Introduction

This chapter explains what is meant by fraud and corruption; terms that are often misunderstood. Straightforward descriptions of the basic conditions that give rise to fraud and corruption are given and the special requirements of the public sector are emphasized.

The bulk of this chapter deals with legal and professional requirements and the basic regulatory framework that applies to most public bodies. Key aspects of regulatory control are explained in detail. The chapter emphasizes the importance of achieving a regulatory framework relevant to operational rather than to strategic considerations. Operational regulations can be particularly useful to the manager by helping to prevent fraud and corruption from becoming established in the workplace.

The chapter finishes with a detailed case study outlining the effects of a poor reporting structure and inadequate internal regulation on one key part of an organization. The general conclusions which are drawn can be widely applied.

Basic conditions surrounding fraud and corruption

Fraud and corruption occur when the two following basic conditions exist.

Intent

There must be intent in the mind of the perpetrator. Intent may arise from a great variety of causes and whether these originate from within the person or from the person's environment makes no practical difference in most situations.

Opportunity

There must be opportunity to perpetrate a corrupt or fraudulent act. An opportunity may be created after being planned and contrived at great length, or it may arise from a chance taken in a passing moment.

Intent

Intent is given relatively limited attention throughout this book. This is because intent is more the specialist realm of the criminologist and criminal psychologist than the auditor, accountant or manager. However, behind intentions lie motivations which can, if recognized in time, indicate the likelihood of fraud and perhaps prevent it occurring.

Table 1.1 Motivations towards fraud and corruption

Personal financial problems: particularly indebtedness, family and gambling-related problems. This category is often the most complex and difficult to recognize. Circumstances that are completely beyond the tolerance of one individual may be considered quite a minor problem by others.

A corporate ethos conducive to corruption: the 'everyone-else-is-doing-it' syndrome. This category may be relatively easy to recognize – overtime 'fiddles', petty pilfering and so on – but is often very difficult to correct. In general corrective action must be firmly taken from the top down.

Disgruntlement and malice: all but the smallest organization will have rivalries and 'co-operation' problems. These can get out of hand and bureaucratic point-scoring can become personal. Officers who feel they have been wronged may try to get even. Also in this category come a wide variety of the under-rewarded pay and 'perks' motivations, particularly if these have persisted for long periods of time.

Ego beating the system by perpetrating fraud can represent a challenge, particularly in the area of computer-related fraud discussed in Chapter 5.

Peer pressure: this is effectively part of the corporate culture category. But with peer groups the pressures are usually more intensive and restricted to parts of an organization.

Ideological: these include political, even religious motivations. Also in this category (and possibly partly under 'Ego') can be placed 'Robin Hood' motivations of fraud to redistribute wealth from the rich to the poor, usually including the perpetrator.

Motivations can be extremely complex and because of this they are usually easier to recognize with hindsight than before the event. Nevertheless, because they can provide a useful warning signal, they are worth considering in broad outline.

Table 1.1 outlines some of the more commonly mentioned motivations. Each one is a genuine cause of concern whether or not it becomes the cause of intent to perpetrate fraud or corruption. Most auditors and senior managers would take notice of these motivations and try, informally at least, to bring them to the attention of other senior managers, or trained counselling staff. Often the manager or auditor will be able to discuss his or her concerns directly with the officers affected. If this is done in time, managers may be able to 'cure' these adverse motivating factors which, after all, is no more than sound management practice.

These motivations or causes of intent could be subdivided and reclassified to seemingly unlimited extents. Beyond this the matter of intent becomes a moral issue outside the scope of this work.

Opportunity

Opportunity, unlike intent, is very much the concern of this book. In particular many of the techniques outlined and cases discussed seek to enable the auditor and more often the manager to minimize opportunity for fraud and corruption.

Opportunities can arise from almost any conditions. Long-term stability can lead to complacency – 'Joe always uses the same route to the bank... the same computer password... the same firm of contractors... etc.' Change can also lead to opportunities, often arising from confusion – 'No one told us who was actually responsible for the bank reconciliation of the new accounts... what exemption would apply to religious orders under the new benefit rules... etc.' Changes in personnel, changes in location, account codes, indeed almost any change of a manual or computerized nature can present opportunities that previously were absent. The regulations, system controls, relationships, attitudes and awareness needed to minimize these opportunities are explained in this book.

Corruption is usually less tangible than fraud. It is a state of mind or ethos that can spread among individuals that make up an organization. Corruption can lead to fraud which is but one of the effects caused by corruption. From an audit viewpoint corruption is more complex than fraud.

Evidence

The conditions surrounding fraud can be complex but in most cases recorded evidence of a fraud exists. For the fraud to remain undetected evidence must be hidden directly by concealment, or indirectly by falsifying records and even the appearance of physical artifacts. For example:

- accounts may contain false entries or be left uncompleted;
- reconciliations may be 'faked';
- stock records may remain unchecked or contain false entries;
- inferior items may be substituted for genuine articles;
- crucial documents may 'go missing'.

Evidence, and how it has been concealed or falsified, will form much of the discussion in later case studies. The recurring question that must be addressed is whether managers can make the evidence of actions and the effects they cause available and 'visible'? For the auditor availability ensures an 'audit trail' and for the manager it ensures responsibility and accountability for the work undertaken.

Such a trail of responsibility shown by written authorizations, well-defined duties, allocation of performance targets, computer passwords or other means, usually enhances quality of output and service. Poor quality is often, but not always, indicative of lax control which may in turn provide opportunity for fraud.

The greater complexity surrounding corruption arises because whereas an effective fraudster may conceal evidence, corruption can occur without generating evidence in the first place. This makes detection during routine audit almost impossible.

The quantifiable extent of fraud is sometimes estimated by writers who refer to types of fraud (e.g. computer fraud) or to geographical areas (e.g. USA, UK, the city of London). Examples include the Audit Commission survey of computer fraud which is done approximately every three years (see Bibliography). Occasionally fraud crime statistics are published on an industrial sector basis. By contrast no one has yet made a realistic attempt to quantify the extent of corruption by reference to value or frequency of occurrence. The most that can be assumed is that the known cases of fraud form but part of the total illegal or unjust actions of corrupt individuals. Favouritism is one of the main manifestations of corruption that goes unrecorded, even at times unnoticed.

Recruitment, promotion, redundancy (or remission therefrom) are oft cited activities where favouritism can play a determining part. Beyond these lie the generally more serious examples involving the awarding of major contracts.

Favouritism often goes hand in hand with bribery, also largely unrecorded, though favouritism may arise from family or social connections in which the pecuniary interest is often difficult to ascertain.

Corruption and the funding of public bodies

Corruption in a public sector body may not be seen as such in the private sector. Who could call a father corrupt for favouring the employment of, or awarding of contracts to, his son or daughter in the context of a family business? Such is generally acceptable custom in society. The critical difference is one of ownership.

The owner, or major shareholder with a controlling interest, is acting on his own behalf and in his own interests. The public servant is acting on behalf of the taxpayers or their elected representatives. The large public corporation is analogous to the public sector in this respect; its share capital is often diffused among thousands of individuals and other organizations and sometimes ultimate ownership is difficult to disentangle among complex intercompany holdings, though the analogy begins to break down when possible liability is considered, as shareholders are not likely to be liable for more than the share value, whereas taxpayers often have to foot virtually the whole bill for fraudulent or corrupt public officials. But in any situation, public or private sector, an employee is generally held to act corruptly when putting personal gain before public or corporate interests in his professional decision-making capacity.

This commonly-held professional ethic can, it would seem, be remarkably difficult to remember in the heady atmosphere surrounding major financial decisions. Some of the cases illustrated later in this book revolve around this problem.

Funders of commercial enterprises have the option of avoiding or withdrawing their funding from an enterprise they consider to be run corruptly; funders of public bodies, i.e., taxpayers, do not have such an option. In these circumstances it is hardly surprising that the law recognizes the particular responsibilities of public servants to be seen to be above suspicion of corruption, as we shall discuss below.

The law

Many people are surprised to find that no effective definition of fraud can be gleaned from English law. Fraud is more of a generic term. It is used to describe any significant and deliberate misrepresentation of financial affairs for the benefit of the perpetrator, or others for whom the perpetrator is acting, possibly without their knowledge. For practical purposes almost any definition of fraud and corruption is likely to be inadequate, or far too long for convenient recall. The act of intentional deception by the perpetrator distinguishes fraud from common error but obtaining proof of intention is usually one of the most difficult aspects of a fraud investigation.

English law is a mixture of statute and common law, that is, law made by Parliament and law arising from precedents set by judicial decisions. Not only are we faced with a lack of legal definition of fraud, though corruption is better defined, but not all criminal law that could relate to fraud is recorded in statute. In 1965 the Law Commission was set up and it has attempted to codify much of the common law, particularly that relating to criminal law, and many of the statutes in the fraud section of Table 1.2 arise from this work. Nevertheless this level of codification is complex and means that unless an auditor is to specialize in regulatory audit or 'audit law', legal advice will almost certainly be required at the first signs of potential criminal prosecution.

Corruption causes particular concern in public bodies. The prevention of corruption or any **suspicion** of corruption is generally a matter of great political significance whatever may or may not be proved in a court of law. History is not short of examples of politicians being forced to resign amid allegation of fraud or corruption.

Local government law in particular requires members and officers to declare any interest in dealings with companies. This is often a crucial requirement in preventing corruption during capital works contracts as Chapter 4 reveals. In general, if an officer can be shown to have accepted or to have agreed to accept any gift or inducement, he is almost certain to be considered guilty of an offence. Such action, in serious cases, can lead to imprisonment as well as a fine and even relatively modest inducements may lead to serious disciplinary action. In fact the public sector employee has often virtually to assume he will be considered guilty unless he can prove his innocence: 'any money, gift or

Table 1.2 Relevant statutes

Corruption
  Prevention of Corruption Acts 1906, 1916 and 1972
  Public Bodies Corrupt Practices Act 1889

Fraud (theft, false accounting, crime and attempted crime)
  Theft Acts 1968 and 1978
  Criminal Law Acts 1967 and 1977
  Criminal Damage Act 1971
  Criminal Attempts Act 1981
  Prevention of Fraud (Investments) Act 1958 (sp S13)
  Local Government Act 1972 (sp S95 and 117)

Forgery
  Forgery Act 1913
  Criminal Law Act 1977
  Forgery and Counterfeiting Act 1981

Computer-related (see Chapter 5)
  Data Protection Act 1984
  Computer Misuse Act 1990
  Copyright, Designs and Patents Act 1988

Selected extracts from these acts are given in Appendix 1.1

consideration paid or received shall be deemed to have been paid or received corruptly as an inducement or reward unless the contrary is proved' (CIPFA Financial Information Service p. 280). See also the Prevention of Corruption Act 1916, Section 2 of which is reproduced in Appendix 1.1.

The law relating to forgery is in some ways even stricter than law relating to fraud. Forgery may be committed even though the 'forged' items have not been used and, perhaps, no intention to use them for financial gain can be proved. Thus the act of reproducing, say, a licence may be an offence in circumstances where it cannot be proved when, or indeed how, its use was intended.

Over the past decade legislation has been enacted to deal specifically with the startling increase in computer-related crime. The Computer Misuse Act 1990 is the most directly relevant of the three acts listed in Table 1.2 and these will be discussed in more detail in Chapter 5.

Professional accounting guidelines

The Chartered Institute of Public Finance and Accountancy (CIPFA) define fraud as: 'Those intentional distortions of financial statements or other records which are carried out to conceal the misappropriation of assets or otherwise for gain' (see Further reading). Fraud is always intentional and dishonest and CIPFA's definition does at least seem to convey this message.

The following is an essentially external auditors' definition. The Auditing Practices Committee, now superseded by the Auditing Practices Board (APB), states: 'fraud… involves the use of deception to obtain an unjust or illegal financial advantage;'

From the Auditing Guideline – 'The auditors' responsibility in relation to fraud, other irregularities and errors' (see Further reading).

The Audit Commission's Code of Practice (1983) (see Further reading) defines fraud very widely indeed as 'any intentional misrepresentation of financial information'. Many public bodies and programmes are after all set up for the very purpose of remedying what is perceived as an injustice and any misrepresentations might arouse great public interest.

Applying the professional accounting guidelines

The APB's auditing guidelines are meant to be followed by all qualified members of CCAB accountancy bodies but the one quoted above may not have been drafted with the public sector clearly in mind.

The auditor is being asked not merely to consider any 'illegality' but also any 'injustice', a much wider term, in the above definition. What, after all, is an 'unjust' financial advantage?

The APB's definition seems to imply that, 'unjust' and 'illegal' will coincide. This may not, on reflection, be surprising. Few private sector auditors would consider qualifying an external audit report on the grounds that certain transactions, although perfectly legal, may be thought unjust. Exceptions might occur at the margin where the law is unclear but, unless the amounts are material in relation to a company's accounts, legality and justice will usually be taken as synonymous. But for the public sector auditor 'unjust' can have far wider implications of public interest.

Questions of justice open up areas of political debate that are the realm of the elected politician rather than the auditor or the manager. But whatever political decisions are made, detailed regulations and day-to-day judgements also have to be made by officers. Although it must be expected that no bribes are accepted to bend the rules, an officer may still have a great deal of discretion to act 'justly', or not. Benefit assessments, property valuations, grants for worthy local causes and other discretionary expenditure all require an element of interpretation and judgement. A wide variety of statistics and financial figures must be presented to political decision-makers, often organizations or individuals who may have a degree of vested interest in the outcome. Senior management is generally expected to ensure that such figures are not misrepresentations. Detailed and complex regulations must be drafted to apply, sometimes nationally sometimes locally, in a wide variety of circumstances. Individual cases and claims must be examined in the light of these regulations. Decisions to allow, amend, impose a penalty, prosecute, etc., must be made. The APB's term, 'justice' and the Audit Commission's term 'misrepresentations' are, in such circumstances, subject to political sensitivity rather than being merely a matter of what the law will allow.

Internal regulations

Well-framed internal regulations usually play a passive yet vital role in preventing, or at least substantially reducing, fraud and corruption. Badly framed internal regulations can be worse than useless, possibly encouraging a widespread attitude of contempt for honesty and consistency in dealings throughout the organization.

Regulations that guard against fraud and corruption are generally included in laid-down financial procedures, though general management regulations (particularly in respect of recruitment, promotion, discipline and relationships with outside bodies) may also be relevant. Internal regulations come under a wide variety of headings: 'financial regulations' and 'standing orders' are used in many local and health authorities; 'government accounting' is a widely used set of accounting regulations applying to the civil service. These are often supplemented by additional departmental or trading unit's own instructions. Whatever the name, certain key features are generally applicable to regulations designed to guard against fraud and corruption. For convenience these have been classified under the headings of content, responsibility, unforeseen events, style, regulations required under higher authority, arbitration and relevance.

Content

All areas of financial and related procedures of a regular on-going nature must be included. For example:

- cash collection procedures
- banking arrangements
- budgetary controls and financial planning
- stocktaking and stores accounting
- insurance arrangements
- ordering and procurement procedures
- payment procedures including sundry creditors
- investments and lending controls
- borrowing controls
- setting and collection of fees and charges
- payment of allowances for subsistence, etc.
- salaries and wages payments
- bonus, commission and overtime payments
- estates management accounting
- audit arrangements, internal and external
- bookkeeping and recording
- accounting arrangements, financial and management
- security of value stocks
- inventory preparation
- virement
- loans fund operations
- appointment of consultants
- contract letting arrangements
- pensions and superannuation

- debt raising, write-off and cancellation
- year-end accounting arrangements
- grant accounting and recording
- revenue (tax, charge, etc.) variation approvals
- financial appraisal procedures
- anticompetitive practices.

Such lists will, of course, vary greatly between bodies according to the nature of their work. Most, for example, will have regulations governing banking, book-keeping, financial accounting and audit. Virement is more appropriate to central and local government, and this is discussed in Chapter 9. Many bodies will not be sufficiently large to warrant a loans fund. Grant accounting regulations may pertain to 'grant-in-aid' monies used to fund a central government function or grants given by local authorities to fund a local charity or other voluntary body. The important point, when framing the regulations, is that all on-going areas of financial significance are covered.

Responsibility

Responsibilities must be clearly set out. Phrases such as 'subject to general agreement', or 'in accordance with accepted practice' should be avoided. Responsibilities should be clearly seen to be allocated to individual senior managers; or to definite departmental duties which are easily and unambiguously recognized as the responsibility of a departmental head; or, if considered to be particularly sensitive, to committees of elected members.

Unforeseen events

Wherever possible contingency should be made for unforeseen events, especially events that make it impossible for a regulation to be followed without conflicting with other higher regulations or acting directly counter to the interests of the organization. Provisions should be made for a timely written explanation, to be reported by named officers, to the appropriate minister, board, elected members or similar level, setting out the reasons for the regulation(s) being waived.

Style

The regulations should be clearly numbered and kept as short as possible. They should be written in a house style commonly used throughout the organization in reports and memoranda. The contents should be summarized at the start and each section should be headed up in a clear and precise manner.

Regulations required under higher authority

Whenever internal regulations are made under a statutory or other require-ment this should be noted and a suitable reference included.

Arbitration

Any agreed authority for arbitration of disputes arising from conflicting interpretations of the regulations should be made clear.

Relevance

Regulations should be kept regularly under review by those responsible for their drafting and/or enforcement. Usually this involves senior financial managers and auditors. Updating should be undertaken so that relevance to operational circumstances and system changes is maintained. All those likely to be affected by changes should be kept fully informed, in writing, quoting the precise amendments made.

'Desk' instructions and other specialized regulations

These instructions refer to particular areas or activities of the public body, rather than to the body as a whole. They are commonly overlooked in works on fraud and corruption. At best 'desk' instructions are given relatively short shrift in internal reviews of organization-wide instructions. Two likely reasons for this lack of consideration are, firstly, that such instructions can be of immense diversity even within any one organization and secondly, that they are sometimes drafted at a relatively junior rank. These circumstances may create a general impression that 'desk' instructions do not really matter very much. On the contrary, when it comes to matters of fraud and corruption nothing could be further from the truth.

Managers cannot usually be expected to give high priority to reviewing 'desk' instructions during day-to-day operations, when their minds are concentrated on clearing a backlog in transactions or on similar operational pressures. Unfortunately desk instructions tend to get the urgent attention they usually need only 'after the horse has bolted': perhaps after a high value cheque has failed to clear or after blank cheques that were not locked safely away were stolen and cleared through the organization's account.

Important internal controls (see Chapter 3) are often written into desk instructions such as requirements for cheques to be countersigned or duties to be performed by separate officers who are specifically mentioned. Sometimes poor, or completely absent, desk instructions can indicate areas of serious system weaknesses.

Auditors should generally ask to see and should review desk instructions during each major audit assignment. If none are available or can be easily found this should be noted. The latter stages of an audit visit are often a suitable time to raise the issue of poor desk instructions. The auditor will have gained greater insight into the current system towards the end of the audit and can make more useful suggestions for expanding, contracting, or otherwise improving the desk instructions.

The points relating to internal regulations for the whole organization should also be applied to desk instructions such as operational manuals, workshop rules, etc. Even though the auditor cannot be expected to be familiar with every page of an organization's desk instructions he or she should review their general relevance to the operational procedures and to any transactions that are processed. The managers should ensure that arrangements for updating and review are adequate and that all officers and staff likely to need to refer to desk instructions have copies. This latter point is particularly important where staff are relatively inexperienced and may need to deal with unfamiliar circumstances.

Responsibilities for investigation

A persistent debate, sometimes strident, more usually rumbling along, has dogged relationships between auditors and managers. The arguments in this debate revolve around the precise roles and duties of each party in relation to fraud and corruption, and more particularly who should take responsibility for investigation, at least until matters are handed over to the police.

Current legal and professional precedents leave little doubt that management bears the main responsibility for ensuring that reasonable measures are taken to prevent fraud and corruption. It is usually to management that occurrences or suspicions of malpractice are first reported. Yet, sometimes the auditor may be approached by parties who know, or suspect, that management is implicated in a malpractice.

In any event it is common practice for managers to request assistance and advice from auditors upon suspicion or discovery of fraud. In some circumstances managers prefer to involve auditors in investigations to make it plain to all concerned that these are being conducted by an independent third party without, initially at least, involving the police and risking possible criminal proceedings.

Many cases of fraud involve a complicated trail of transactions that line managers and the police would find difficult to unravel. Most auditors are also accountants and are more likely to be able to deal with such situations.

There is little doubt that, despite their ultimate responsibility, managers' efforts in respect of investigation generally benefit from the involvement of auditors. This is hardly surprising; apart from what has already been said, auditors direct much of their time and effort towards recommending improvements in internal controls that directly or indirectly guard against fraud and corruption.

It is perhaps because of this very concern with internal controls that an element of confusion arises. A manager may feel, perhaps with some justification, that an auditor who failed to point out serious inadequacies in internal controls in his (the manager's) system should bear some of the blame when these inadequacies enable malpractice.

Nevertheless the final responsibility must lie with managers unless the auditor has given specific assurance regarding specific controls. The analogy is sometimes drawn with the MOT testing of a motor car. If, say, a car is found to have a bald tyre immediately after passing its MOT test, the garage is clearly at fault. If the sun-roof is not working or the tyre is found to be bald 1000 miles or 10 weeks later, the garage is probably in the clear. The auditor must be careful to document carefully all the work he undertakes and especially all the tests he performs. If the auditor checks, say, that orders 1–4 and 15–19 have been agreed to invoices and payments are correctly authorized, within budget and not *ultra vires*, and draws conclusions consistent with this evidence, he or she cannot readily be held responsible for a fraud relating to order No. 6.

Unless a fraud can be shown to relate directly to matters on which the auditor has expressed his views and opinions in a clear manner it is unlikely that the manager can rely on an audit to provide an excuse for not preventing a fraud. Of course many other factors such as collusion between an employee and a claimant may have negated any reasonable steps the manager could have taken.

Interviews

Interviews are an integral part of many fraud investigations. In most situations, particularly when suspicions begin to appear well founded or a fraud has been openly declared, interviews should be conducted by the police, customs officers or others specifically trained to do so. The method of gathering evidence from

Table 1.3 Evidence and Interviews

1. Audit papers and notes should be kept and initialled and dated. This is in any case the usual professional practice. The sources of evidence should be clearly stated even if this is an anonymous tip-off.

2. The papers should be adequate for an intelligent layman to follow the auditor's facts and reasoning to see how he reached his conclusions. In this respect they may need to be more detailed than normal papers which need only be sufficient for another auditor not familiar with the case. All documentary evidence from the clients, or other papers, should be held in original form rather than being copied. Evidence will be indexed and filed so that its purpose and its source can be clearly identified. No original document that may be required as court evidence should remain in use. Copies may be made for the client's purposes.

3. Interviews should be very carefully conducted. At this point it is worth considering calling in the police. They have far more experience of interviewing suspected fraudsters than do auditors. Even so, interviews may be conducted by auditors, perhaps because of the need for urgency or because, originally, fraud was not suspected.

4. The provisions of the Police and Criminal Evidence Act 1984 should be adhered to. No promises or inducements should be made. Suspects must be cautioned along the lines of: 'You do not have to say anything unless you wish to do so, but whatever you say may be given in evidence.'

5. The interviewee must be told that he or she is not under arrest, is not obliged to remain with the interviewer and that if they do remain they may obtain legal advice if they wish to.

6. Interviewing should be conducted with at least two auditors present, at least one of whom should be of the same sex as the suspect. Notes should be made during the course of the interview stating the place and time of commencement and termination. The names of those present should also be recorded.

7. At the conclusion of the interview the interviewee should be allowed to read the record made and record any points of disagreement he/she has.

8. If a person wishes to write his or her own statement or record, he or she should be asked to write and sign and date the following prior to making their written statement: 'I make this statement of my own free will. I understand that I need not say anything unless I wish to do so and that what I say may be given in evidence.'

9. In all but the most exceptional circumstances auditors will have been able to call upon the assistance of the police prior to conducting such an interview.

(Reproduced by permission from P. Jones and J. Bates *Public Sector Auditing: Practical Techniques for an Integrated Approach*, Chapman and Hall, 1990.)

interviews requires particular care, otherwise efforts may be wasted in terms of any successful prosecution. Even if a prosecution is not envisaged evidence must be gathered objectively, systematically, and in a well-documented manner. This is usually consistent with good audit practice and reinforces the points made above regarding the need for audit involvement.

At times events may overtake the auditor's or manager's practical ability to call in the police. A routine audit may reveal the possibility of fraud which requires investigation before, say, funds are due to be transferred abroad or the prime suspect is due to take a holiday. Sometimes a routine interview regarding some apparently innocent errors elicit unexpectedly an admission of wrongdoing. In any event it is unlikely that management or auditors would call in an outside agency before any in-house work had been undertaken to establish the initial facts. These can be sensitive times for all concerned and Table 1.3 sets out some of the more important points of which to be aware.

The points set out are, it must be stressed, no substitute whatsoever for adequate training and awareness of important details such as the Police and Criminal Evidence Act 1984.

Summary

This chapter has outlined important legal and professional interpretations of fraud and corruption. Although precise definition of fraud is difficult its general nature should be apparent and specific instances will be clarified further as this book progresses, particularly in the case studies. The basic environment surrounding fraud and corruption has been outlined in terms of the two prime conditions of opportunity and intent.

A regulatory hierarchy has been outlined. This hierarchy is one of descending authority and precedence, but not necessarily of descending

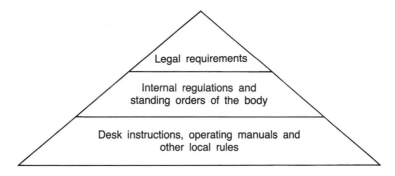

Figure 1.1 Regulatory hierarchy

relevance and 'usefulness' in preventing fraud and corruption, as shown in Figure 1.1.

Responsibilities for investigation and interviews are subject to some debate. But in all circumstances a degree of caution is required and fraud interviews should be handled by trained police or others familiar with the Police and Criminal Evidence Act.

Case study

This, the first case study, illustrates how lax instructions encourage poor internal control in terms of both procedures and of organizational structure. It also outlines a situation where an auditor and manager deal with the urgent need to improve both standing orders and desk instructions.

Case study 1.1 Toxins Research and Storage Centre (TRSC)

Background

TRSC is a small outstation of a major government ministry employing 29 scientific and 15 security, administrative and manual staff. They carry out vital military research involving chemical agents. The high–security facilities make TRSC a suitable temporary depository for storing dangerous substances, sometimes on behalf of civil authorities such as police or customs officers.

TRSC forms part of the cyclical audit strategy of the ministry's internal audit. Total expenditure was considered to be relatively low in relation to similar cyclical responsibilities, currently £700 500 p.a. and income, from recharging for storage, was generally only around £15 000–£16 000 p.a. No significant financial risk factors were known to exist and TRSC was classified for audit purposes as a low materiality, low risk establishment, to be visited approximately every three years.

Summary of events

The audit proceeded smoothly until a serious fraud was uncovered. Income, it appeared, should have far exceeded that recorded in the books. The main sequence of events was as follows.

During the audit several comments were made to the auditor to the effect that extra storage space was urgently required. The administration manager, who doubled as finance officer for the site, stressed that they were having to turn away shipments from civil authorities worth approximately £500 per month in storage charges. A senior scientific officer hinted that someone, i.e. the auditor, should undertake a value-for-money (VFM) investigation into the financial returns that could be gained from 'investing' in an adjacent site of waste land owned by a local farmer.

The auditor was puzzled. He had at no time budgeted for VFM work (and in any case he had heard that the local farmer was the father of the senior scientific officer whose judgments in the matter might not be completely unbiased). But more importantly his experience of similar sites indicated that, for the number of deliveries, income was low. Also, he was not aware of any similar problem at two other research stations he had visited recently, both with storage facilities of about the same capacity.

A relatively brief analytical review of income confirmed his worst fears as follows. The average container size (area only, no 'stacking' was allowed) was $10 \text{ m} \times 4 \text{ m} = 40 \text{ m}^2$. Containers were sometimes hired from outside companies, sometimes they were those specially constructed by the ministry. The capacity of the yard was 4500 m^2.

The manager's personal impression was that the yard rarely had more than 200 m^2 of space unused. A brief review of the past month's records of deliveries and containers in stock confirmed this. The auditor, to err on the prudent side in his estimate, allowed for 500 m^2 of unused capacity.

Storage charges had been set at £1.00 per m^2 per week for the past year.

It was immediately clear that if only, say, 4000 m^2 of space capacity was used up, for the entire year income would amount to $4000 \times £1.00 \times 52 = £208\,000$. This was so far in excess of actual income that even allowing for slumps in demand, suspicion of serious misstatements if not false accounting and fraud was warranted. Further investigation led eventually to the dismissal of the manager in charge of stores and his conviction, together with the employees of outside hauliers, on criminal charges involving theft, forgery and false accounting.

The basic weaknesses were:

1. lack of any reasonable separation of duties due to an undue concentration of responsibilities in the hands of the single stores manager;
2. a complete absence of any checking by more senior or independent officers.

The stores manager's position in the organization's hierarchy is shown in Figure 1.2

Nominally the stores manager, although relatively low down in the hierarchy, reported directly to the very much more senior administration and finance manager. In practice this link was difficult to maintain as the administration and finance manager had far more senior officers than the stores manager also demanding his attention. Also, in practice, the finance and administration side of the organization placed few demands upon stores whereas the scientific side were the effective stores users. This meant that an 'unofficial' reporting link had arisen from the stores manager to one of the higher scientific officers (HSO) who acted on

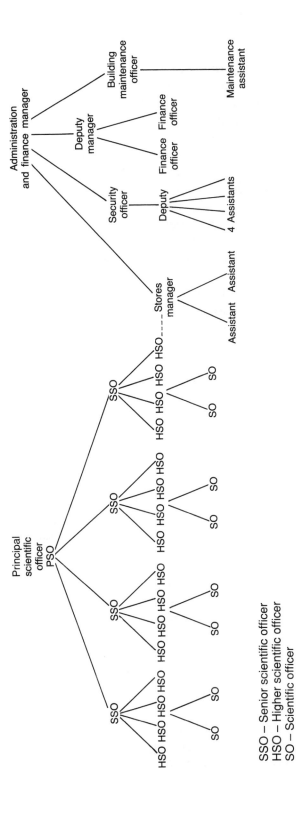

Figure 1.2

SSO – Senior scientific officer
HSO – Higher scientific officer
SO – Scientific officer

behalf of the scientific side to avoid the cumbersome procedure of making requests up one side of the hierarchy via the principal scientific officer. and then down the other side via the administration and finance manager. These arrangements meant that the organization structure enabled the stores manager to operate virtually unsupervised as a free agent within the organization.

All deliveries of containers (and any other consumables such as laboratory or office equipment) were authorized and controlled by the stores manager, usually on the basis of verbal requests from the HEO. Returns of containers and any other movements in and out of the yard were also controlled by the stores manager.

No trading accounts were prepared for TRSC and so the value of stock was of little significance from a financial accounting viewpoint. Stock checks were rarely carried out and those that were undertaken were the sole responsibility of the stores manager rather than an independent officer. A previous auditor had mentioned the poor quality of the annual stock check record and stores records generally. However management was not inclined to treat the matter seriously as these records had, it was thought, little financial or operational significance in terms of performance. The deputy administration and finance officer had said at the time of the visit, 'I don't think anyone will be inclined to steal the stuff we have in stock – I'm more worried about the possibility of a terrorist bomb attack.'

The stores manager had realised several years ago that the yard was rarely used beyond 50% of its capacity. It was also well known to him that storage of dangerous chemicals particularly from industrial waste products was an expensive business. Initially he had offered his 'services' to small hard pressed firms with expensive waste to store or dispose of. TRSC had special high–security disposal arrangements and the stores manager had access to the necessary documentation and could arrange for authorization for disposal, either by himself or by the unsuspecting HEO with whom he liaised. The presence of extra containers caused no suspicion, especially as before long they appeared to come from the same firms on a regular basis. In fact the stores manager usually arranged for the fraudulent deliveries to be let in through the gate by personally notifying the security officer on duty.

Corrective regulatory action

The administration and finance manager and the auditor reviewed the internal regulations of TRSC together with current operational practices and agreed on the following changes.

Revised regulation

*Regulation 4.2. Deliveries
of goods, equipment, parcels
(non Post Office) etc.*

4.2.1

All deliveries must be agreed
to pre-arranged notification
by one of the following officers
prior to entry on site.
PSO – A. B. JOHNSON
SSO – C. D. SMITH
SSO – E. F. BROWN
SSO – G. H. BLACK
HEO – I. J. JONES
Administration Manager: K. L. Jones
Deputy Admin. Manager: M. N. Smith

4.2.2

In the case of any query
A. B. Johnson or K. L. Jones must
agree all inbound deliveries.

*Financial Regulation 1.6.
Stocktaking records*

1.6.1 The stores manager shall
be responsible for the care,
custody and recording of all
stores items held in the main
store room or the adjacent yard.

1.6.2 All stock records shall be
in a form approved by the
administration and finance
manager – K. L. Jones.

1.6.3 All stock movements (goods
received, issues and returns) shall
be initialled by the stores manager

Original regulation

*Regulation 4.2. Deliveries of
goods, equipment, parcels,
(non Post Office) etc.*

4.2.1

All deliveries must be agreed
with an appropriate officer
prior to entry on site.

Internal regulations did not
provide for stocktaking
records.

On searching the existing
regulations the manager
noticed that the only reference to stores records was
in Regulation 1.4.3, under
'year end accounting'
which stated that 'the
officer in charge of stores
shall tabulate all stores of
value as at 31 March of
each year.'

or the assistant on duty in the
space provided on the relevant form.

1.6.4 Issues will only be made on
receipt of an official requisition
authorized by an officer at HEO
level or above.

1.6.5 All write-offs of obsolescent
or damaged stocks must be
approved in writing by the
administration and finance
manager.

Financial Regulation 1.7.
Stock checking procedures.

1.7.1 An annual check of all stock
shall take place during a
convenient weekend as close
as possible to the financial year
end. This work is to be undertaken
by officers delegated by the PSO
and the administration and finance
officer. During this stock check
the stores shall be closed but the
stores manager will be on hand
to answer any queries.

1.7.2 During the annual stock check
the stores manager and his assistants
shall not undertake any official
duties other than to answer queries
as allowed under 1.7.1.

1.7.3 The on-going independent
checking of stock shall be arranged
in addition to measures at 1.7.1 at
the discretion of the PSO.

1.7.4 All stock checking procedures
shall be recorded and evidenced by
the initials of the officers taking
part on records approved by the
finance and administration manager.

Financial Regulation 1.7.
Stock checking procedures.

1.7.1 An annual stock check
will be undertaken as at
31 March each year. The
stores manager may, if he
considers it necessary, close
down normal stores
operations during the period
of the stock check.

The manager and auditor also agreed that in future the day-to-day line of reporting should be from the stores manager to a senior scientific officer (SSO). Although all stores-related financial procedures and records would still be the ultimate responsibility of the administration and finance manager, operational matters such as day-to-day deliveries, issues and movements were determined by the needs of the scientists. Also such matters as stores opening and closing times and the physical storage arrangements were determined largely by scientific officers' needs. Thus, finance officers would need to be satisfied that the checking, costing and recording of items was being undertaken to their requirements while the actual daily stores operation would meet the requirements of the scientific officers.

Separation of duties between requisitioning and ordering movements (scientists); custody (stores officers); and checking/recording (finance officers in conjunction with scientists) would be a significant improvement. These measures, including supervision by the SSO, should ensure no repetition of unauthorised 'independent services' being provided. The improved stock checking and recording requirements should also ensure that risk of any pilferage (though thought unlikely) is reduced to an absolute minimum.

In all probability internal regulations of such poor quality as those of TRSC would need substantial revision. At first sight officers will often question the apparent increase in complexity arising from such circumstances. This complexity is often far less than first impressions indicate. As a general rule revised regulations should not impose extra duties on officers unless, as in the case of TRSC stock checks, these have been agreed as being required to meet management (rather than audit) requirements.

Concluding points

Although no manager or auditor can be continuously aware of what good or evil motivations may be in people's minds, or how these may arise from their environment, he or she should not assume that good intentions will *always* exist. Well-drafted internal regulations, like the adequate internal controls discussed later in this book, should minimize temptations and allow both managers and those they manage to be reasonably assured of an acceptable environment and honest intentions.

A regulatory framework should, ideally, be detailed, flexible, show as clearly as possible where responsibilities lie and at the same time be unobtrusive. In this way people will adhere to acceptable regulations almost by second nature, rather than by effort.

Appendix 1.1

Extracts chosen from Statutes.

Theft Act 1968

This is a basic piece of legislation with some very important definitions. A full reading of the act is recommended to obtain any significant legal appreciation of the definitions extracted.

Theft

S1 'A person is guilty of theft if he dishonestly appropriates property belonging to another with the intention of permanently depriving another of it...'
The act carries on to define 'dishonest', 'appropriate' and 'property'.

S11 is often of particular interest to public sector organizations which contain areas open without restriction to attract members of the public free of charge such as museums, galleries, council meetings or parks.
S11 '...any person who without lawful authority removes from the building or its grounds the whole or part of any article displayed or kept for display to the public... shall be guilty of an offence.'

Under fraud and blackmail the act defines the following:

Obtaining property by deception
S15 'A person who by any deception dishonestly detains the property belonging to another with the intention of permanently depriving the other of it, shall...be liable to imprisonment for a term not exceeding ten years.'

Obtaining pecuniary advantage by deception
S16(i) 'A person who by any deception dishonestly obtains for himself or another any pecuniary advantage shall... be liable to imprisonment for a term not exceeding five years.'

The act defines pecuniary advantage as an evasion of or a reduction in debt, being allowed to borrow or take out insurance or annuity or being allowed to earn remuneration or greater remuneration or to win money by betting.

False accounting
S17 'Where a person dishonestly, with a view to gain for himself or another or with intent to cause loss to another,

(a) destroys, defaces, conceals or falsifies any account or any record or document made or required for any accounting purpose or;
(b) in furnishing information for any purpose produces or makes use of any accounts, or any such record or document as aforesaid, which to his knowledge is or may be misleading, false or deceptive in a material particular; he shall... be liable to imprisonment for a term not exceeding seven years.'

Similar provisions cover supression of documents under S20, also for a term of seven years.

Blackmail
S22 'A person is guilty of blackmail if, with a view to gain for himself or another or with intent to cause loss to another, he makes any unwarranted demand with menaces; ...'

The act then goes on to define 'unwarranted', and the maximum term of imprisonment is fourteen years.

Theft Act 1978

This effectively replaces S16(2) of the Theft Act 1968.

Obtaining services by deception
S1(i) 'A person who by any deception dishonestly obtains services from another shall be guilty of an offence.'

Prevention of Corruption Act 1916

Presumption of corruption in certain cases (i.e. in public bodies)
S2 'Where in any proceedings against a person for an offence under the Prevention of Corruption Act 1906, or the Public Bodies Corrupt Practices Act 1889, it is proved that any money, gift, or other consideration has been paid or given to or received by a person in the employment of His Majesty or any Government Department or a public body by or from a person, or a guest of a person, holding or seeking to obtain a contract from His Majesty or any Government Department or public body, the money, gift, or consideration shall be deemed to have been paid or given and received corruptly as such inducement or reward as is mentioned in such Act unless the contrary is proved.'

The 1906 Prevention of Corruption Act S1 and the 1889 Public Bodies Corrupt Practices Act S1 and S2

These outline corruption and corrupt transactions in quite comprehensive detail which for the sake of reasonable brevity is not reproduced in full in this appendix.

The 1981 Forgery and Counterfeiting Act

Forgery
S1 'A person is guilty of forgery if he makes a false statement with the intention that he or another shall use it to induce somebody to accept it as genuine, and by reason of so accepting it to do or not to do some act to his own or to any other person's prejudice.'

Copying a false instrument
'It is an offence for a person to make a copy of an instrument which is and which he knows or believes to be, a false instrument...' The act includes further detailed definition of the intention and offences related to using false instruments and particular details relating to money orders, passports, share certificates, etc.

Local Government Act 1972

Disclosure of officers' interests
S117 'If it comes to the knowledge of any officer employed... by a local authority that a contract in which he has any pecuniary intent, whether direct or indirect... has been, or is proposed to be, entered into by the authority or any committee thereof, he shall as soon as practicable give notice in writing to the authority of the fact that he is interested therein.'

Disclosure of political members' interests
S94 '...if a member of a local authority has any pecuniary interest, direct or indirect, in any contract, proposed contract or other matter, and is present at a meeting of the local authority at which the contract or other matter is the subject of consideration he shall at the meeting and as soon as practicable

after its commencement disclose the fact and shall not take part in the consideration or discussion of the contract or any other matter or vote on any question with respect to it.'

The act goes on to define pecuniary interests in some detail. These provisions are given added weight by the Local Government and Housing Act 1989, S19, which gives the Secretary of State powers to require members to give information about their pecuniary interests.

2

The public sector

Introduction

This short chapter has been written to portray the public sector in a wider context than will be possible during the detailed financial and administrative arrangements considered later.

No apologies are made for questioning the very existence of a public sector, nor for digressing from the practical theme of this book into wider historical and public finance issues. We live in an age when the size and extent of the public sector has come under increasing scrutiny from politicians and voters whose queries many readers will, as public servants, be duty bound to consider.

In this chapter broad historical developments are briefly outlined and basic questions concerning the rationale of the public sector are considered, followed by insights from economists and others into the nature of public sector finance. This useful, if basic, background is intended for managers, accountants and auditors who need to understand the special nature of public sector bodies compared to most other organizations, which in turn affects the nature of public sector fraud and corruption.

The public sector – its special nature

Civilized societies have always displayed a public sector. By public sector we usually mean all communally provided goods and services that are paid for by taxation or other revenues raised by law. In a democracy 'raised by law' means revenues raised by common consent, or at least acquiescence; but in any society this revenue-raising function of government is, if necessary, backed up by force or threat of force. An RAF Tornado aircraft and a National Health Service (NHS) funded hospital, for example, are part of the public sector. In contrast a private airline or an unsubsidized health clinic are not part of the public sector, neither is a non-profit-making voluntary charity. Although there will always be areas of doubt such as NHS private beds, three broad distinctions can be drawn on the basis of 'enforceability' of funding. First there is a legally enforced public sector, second a market-driven private sector and third, voluntary clubs or charities.

When we discussed the legal definitions of fraud and corruption in the previous chapter we noted that these are stricter than the general requirements of the Theft Acts. The element of force, or threat of force, that lies behind taxation and the fact that public servants are always dealing with other people's money gives additional weight to the view that public servants have extra requirements to be seen to be honest and fair. The public servant may even be assumed guilty unless he can prove his innocence. The arguments in favour of this state of affairs run something like the following.

A 'master' may choose freely to trust his 'servant' in the private sector world of normal trade and business. That choice is not available to the electorate and public servants cannot simply assume they will be trusted with the funds in their control. They must always be accountable. If, for whatever reason, they cannot account for any losses then the public have a right to assume the worst. In local government this might lead to councillors or officers being surcharged. These arguments go some way to help explain the extra red tape sometimes associated with governments. We shall return to this issue when examining fraud and value for money projects in Chapter 9.

An historical view

Historians would be hard pressed to define accurately the first examples of a public sector; its origins lie in the origins of civilization itself. Ancient public works are well researched by archaeologists. They were often defence or crop related, such as fortifications and irrigation schemes and at the same time they usually owed much to religious organization. Grain stores needed supervision and, no doubt, some method of controlling issues and calling in new stocks. The defensive walls and architectural achievements such as those of the ancient and famous walls of Jericho required public organization, foresight, technical skills and, no doubt, enforced taxation.

The many writings on early civilization and particularly the growth of cities, such as Lewis Mumford's famous work *The City in History*,[1] generally point out the importance of early societies' ability to produce sufficient surpluses. The surpluses of food and wealth were used to support priests, soldiers, craftsmen and others. These surpluses made early societies attractive targets, hence the overriding importance of military works.

The unsung forerunners of today's civil administrators, engineers and accountants have, over thousands of years, supported public sectors that made possible the famous achievements of generals, monarchs and empires. Throughout their long history public officials have, with varying degrees of success, been held to account for their actions by their masters, whoever these were at the time.

Despite such a long historical tradition, it is possible to ignore most of the development of public bodies until relatively recent times and still attempt to understand the emergence of the modern public sector in Great Britain and other similar developed western countries. We can do this largely because the agricultural and industrial revolutions and the associated growth of western-style democracy has, over the past two centuries or so, completely changed the nature of the public sector. Public administrations created to serve monarchic and autocratic societies, based upon overtly military and religious power, have generally been replaced by, or evolved into, bodies created to implement the policies of political parties. A sceptic might add that some of the adaptations have not been wholly successful. But change on such a gigantic scale is seldom without its failures.

The industrial revolution first evolved in Britain. The main developments took place over the period from the eighteenth century onward. Without going into great detail, three broad trends are worth noting from the viewpoint of the development of the public sector:

1. an increasing regulatory role of the state;
2. an increasing level of direct provision, especially welfare;
3. the effects of large-scale wars.

The earliest trend was the increase in administrative and judicial apparatus required to cope with the effects of industry and the related social changes. This trend may be seen as an increase in the regulatory and to a lesser extent the enabling role of the state, both of which are described in more detail later in this chapter. For now we may note that poverty was a major factor inspiring this regulatory expansion, for example the Poor Law Acts, from 1536 right through to the Poor Law Amendment Act of 1834. These acts attempted to deal with the problems accompanying the great social upheavals such as overcrowding and famine caused by, or coinciding with, the agricultural and later the industrial revolution. The Poor Law Acts were followed by the Old Age Pension Act 1908 and the National Insurance Act 1911. Public sector regulatory expansion set the scene and encouraged the expansion of the Welfare State, indicative of the second broad trend. The Welfare State has often usurped the role formerly given to religious and private charities. Charities were totally incapable of dealing with the effects of population growth, urbanization and the disappearance of vast tracts of common land. In many ways local Boards and later Local Authorities filled the demand for social regulation and relief of poverty that the church and the aristocracy could not manage to meet. Welfare in its broadest sense of, say, basic health and education needs, became seen as a right rather than as a reward for service or loyalty. The distinction so often mentioned in the earliest years of the industrial revolution between the deserving and undeserving poor became increasingly blurred.

The original regulatory and enabling role became increasingly one of direct provision and state intervention. Undoubtedly the rise of the Labour Party and British socialism generally did much to encourage the expansion of the Welfare State with the public sector now seen as a direct provider of welfare goods and services.

This providing role may be reducing, collapsing some would say, under the last decade of Conservative policies. But a core of public goods and services such as the housing and care of the very disadvantaged in society seems bound to remain. This is discussed later in the chapter when we consider briefly the views of some public sector economists.

The third basic trend is often described as 'war prompted' expenditure. Whatever the magnitude of expanding regulatory and welfare related expenditure, large scale wars appear to have boosted this trend. After each boost the public expenditure level, though falling back a little, has remained higher than before. This trend is also considered further when we discuss the views of economists.

Before we tackle an economic view and proceed to the practical issues that are the main purpose of this book, further questions concerning the broad nature and development of the modern public sector must be considered – questions which address some basic moral and political issues from which can be gained a wider appreciation of the practical causes of public sector fraud and corruption.

Some basic questions

Perhaps the most important question is this: is a public sector inevitable? This very basic question is of fundamental importance. Although, as we have seen, history seems to support a positive answer, the question should not, on account of this, be side-stepped. In fact an honest official may be concerned with this question not simply to understand the nature of the public sector but to justify his or her employment in its cause.

If it were possible to have an economically productive society with no public sector then taxpayers who would, if given the choice, choose not to use the goods or services provided by the public sector could argue that they were being institutionally robbed. If, however, a public sector is inevitable then such a choice is meaningless for all practical purposes. Those who would indeed choose not to consume any public goods and services might argue that the 'world' was unfair to them but they could not justly point the finger of blame at the public sector or its servants. The public sector, they would be told, exists because the 'world' is the way it is and to avoid this one would first have to change the 'world', i.e. human nature.

If a public sector is inevitable then public servants can be, to varying degrees, merely honest or dishonest; competent or incompetent. The question best asked by the usually hard pressed taxpayer is not 'Am I being robbed?' (i.e. forced to pay for nothing or at best for something I could realistically avoid given the choice) but rather, 'Is what is provided, provided lawfully and justly and is it good value for money?' The answer to this question depends, ultimately, on subjective values such as moral attitudes, conventions of justice and political values. Despite the subjectivity of this answer it is generally possible to make basic assumptions that are acceptable to most people in most situations. From these assumptions it is possible to undertake quite precise checks and measurements. If this was not the case any attempt to combat fraud and corruption would be doomed to failure from the start.

If a public sector is inevitable, what is the basic role of the public sector? For most practical purposes public sector provision tends to take place due to three, slightly overlapping, roles. These roles have been mentioned briefly when we considered the three basic historical trends earlier in the chapter. They are the following.

A regulatory role

This represents the very minimal function of the public sector: regulations are legion in any modern society, from regulation of the airwaves at a national level to regulation of local rights of way.

An enabling role

The ultimate purpose of most regulation can be seen to be an enabling one. Parking restrictions, unpopular though they nearly always are, enable traffic to flow and road safety to be maintained. Often the enabling role demands a more active role by the public sector than simply setting standards and by-laws – compulsory purchase of land for roads, for example, or, more fundamentally, the maintenance of law and order to enable most ordinary life to function unhindered.

Direct provision of goods and services

The enabling role merges, often imperceptibly, into the direct provision of goods and services; low cost social housing and education, for example. Much direct provision is not provision of pure public goods and services, a concept discussed below. Both privatization and compulsory competitive tendering have, in recent years, eaten into the directly providing role of the public sector.

Some services it must be admitted are difficult to categorize. Street lighting, for example, is a directly provided public good but few people 'consume' street lighting for its own sake, rather it enables them to walk safely about their towns and cities for work or pleasure.

Despite some difficult cases the progression from regulatory to direct provision follows a general pattern of increasing administrative and technical complexity in the public bodies set up to undertake the tasks involved. From laying down, say, effluent emission standards to constructing a network of top secret radar defence stations the involvement of the public sector becomes increasingly direct, controlling, complex and generally costly.

An economic view

We mentioned above the term 'pure public goods'. Are some goods and services inherently better in some way when provided by the communal actions of a public sector? This would seem to be implied if a public sector is indeed inevitable. Economists often refer to 'public goods' meaning goods (and presumable services) that the free market fails to provide, at least to a standard considered socially acceptable. The free market may provide defence in the form of mercenaries but – Gurkhas excepted – most modern societies do not rely on mercenaries for defence.

How, then, can we define a 'public good'? Usually it is one that most people say they want but for which no one individual can be readily persuaded to pay. Some examples together with suggested distinguishing characteristics are outlined in Figure 2.1. The last characteristic of Figure 2.1 (column 3) is particularly important for this book. For example, the many

Characteristic / Public good	Once the goods have been provided the exclusion of individual consumers is impossible or not worth the cost 1	Commonly accepted philanthropic values exist 2	Risk of corruption is very high under free market provision 3
Defence	✓		✓
Roads	✓		
Streetlights	✓		
Means-tested benefit		✓	✓
Police force	✓	✓	✓
Fire service	✓		✓
Health, etc. inspectors	✓		✓
Road traffic safety campaign	✓	✓	
Judges			✓

Figure 2.1

government inspectors of health, schools, safety, pollution, etc. must be paid by an independent and largely incorruptible body (even if its employees are not all incorruptible). Consider, say, a private health inspectorate that found one of its major 'clients' provided food from disease infected kitchens. Could it afford to lose its client (and its income) by closing the client down, or causing it to go into bankruptcy by disseminating adverse publicity? Even if an inspectorate were to act in secret, what would happen if the client did not do as ordered? A serious conflict of interest clearly exists. The judiciary is a similar case in point; if judges, like barristers, could be 'employed' by the wealthy how could their verdict be seen to be impartial?

Not only does some level of public sector activity appear inevitable but some goods and services appear more suited to public provision than others. Public bodies have proved capable of adapting to accommodate the drastic upheavals in work practices, politics, population distributions, trade and technology that accompany a shift from pre-industrial to developed society. Often, as we shall discuss, there has been more than a mere reactive accommodation by the public sector.

If we exclude the all pervading state sectors from what remains of the Communist world, one very important question still remains: why have the public sectors of the western developed nations expanded so dramatically since around the middle of this century?

The Thatcherite policies of the British government during the 1980s which have proved popular in many parts of the world, have at most reduced the proportion of gross national product accounted for by the public sector by only a few percentage points.

The growth of public expenditure

Mostly, when economists talk about the public sector they talk in terms of expenditure figures. They encounter many difficulties in defining and measuring public expenditure. Should, for example, the expenditure of nationalized industries and 'quangos' be included in the same way as that of government departments? Governments certainly influence nationalized industries, but compared to departments of state or local authorities, their control over expenditure is quite remote. Transfers between central and local government or subsidies to other bodies, usually in the form of grant aid, should not be double counted. The expenditure of various departmental trading funds can be difficult to class, and complex questions are raised by trading at 'arms length', often by quangos or other semi-autonomous bodies.

Although these problems are interesting they are incidental to the main issues. Variation in methods of measurement may be politically controversial but rarely operates on an historical scale. The causes of growth of expenditure since around 1900 appear to lie more with the changes taking place in the economy and in the size, characteristics and expectations of the population.

Public expenditure is often measured as a proportion of gross national product (GNP). GNP is the national output including the costs of capital consumption or replacement and the value of overseas output. Statistics of this magnitude are invariably subject to inaccuracies but virtually all published sources show a marked increase in public expenditure around the late 1940s and into the 1950s to around 40% of GNP and to nearer 50% for much of the late 1970s, falling back to around 40% by the late 1980s. This compares to generally less than 30% in the inter-war years and less than 20% throughout the 1800s and early 1900s. In fact public expenditure is put at only 8% of GNP in 1890 and 12% in 1910.

Over the past 200 years the growth in social services is particularly noticeable as is that of environmental/economic infrastructure. The dominance of central government in terms of expenditure has been significantly challenged by the rise of local government. Central government was the larger during the nineteenth century but the two were virtually neck and neck by 1910; by the early 1980s central government once again held the main share, around 70%, including some areas that had formerly been the responsibility of local government.

A nineteenth-century German economist Wagner[2] propounded what has been called a 'law of increasing state activity' – that government expenditure must increase at a *faster* rate than economic output while countries are undergoing an industrial revolution. This law was based upon empirical observations of the countries of western Europe during the industrial revolution. Wagner's observations pointed to the increasing complexity of economic and social activity such as the increasing division of labour and social friction caused by the stark contrasts of industrial life. Society needed more policing and a more complex legal framework to maintain order (the regulatory role). Large amounts of capital investment in infrastructure, health care and education were demanded by employers and workers (the enabling and providing roles). The free market could not rise to the occasion and meet the new demands and so the nature and scale of the modern public sector emerged.

Some economists, particularly W. W. Rostow,[3] outline a basic model of development stages which help explain the, historically speaking, relative suddenness of economic growth and thereby offer an insight into the expansion of the public sector. Rostow outlined how a traditional society tends to modernize with increasing trade and industrialization until it reaches a critical mass which enables it to take off into sustained growth and eventually reach a stage of economic maturity. These economist's insights into the rise of the industrial revolution and post-industrial revolution society (in Europe and North America at least) fit rather neatly into historical events discussed earlier.

Other economists, notably A. T. Peacock and I. Wiseman[4] in Britain, offered further insights also based largely on empirical observation. The influence of wars in increasing public expenditure and apparently then allowing it to remain at only slightly reduced levels in the following peacetime was noted. The Boer War and, to more noticeable extents, the first and second World Wars show this effect quite starkly.

In peacetime large increases in taxation, certainly if greater than increases in wealth, are unlikely to be acceptable to voters. But in wartime the increased tax burden is accepted for reasons of national survival. After hostilities are over the new obligations of the state tend to persist and any reduction in taxation can be questioned by supporters of various programmes. Wars, it is also argued, tend to focus the government's and voter's attention on social needs that were not so seriously considered during peacetime. Evacuation of children from the cities during World War II is said to have highlighted cases of malnutrition and hitherto largely hidden poverty. Wars are often accompanied by expectations of a 'home fit for heroes' to be built afterwards.

Welfare theorists such as Pigou[5] and Dalton have pointed out that the natural or logical outcome of free choice is for voters to demand a level of public expenditure such that the net benefit from the last or 'marginal' pound of taxation would equal the marginal cost to the taxpayers. Ideally, such theorists maintain, the marginal utility of each type of government expenditure should be the same. Governments should divide their spending such that the net utility of an extra pound spent on, say, roads was the same as that spent on, say, hospitals.

J. M. Keynes[6] and other economists expanded ideas which, grossly simplified, were taken by politicians to justify large-scale attempts at managing the national economy. Terms such as 'demand management' and 'pump priming' became fashionable. Government was seen as a controller of the economic machine. 'Demand', the economists' common soup of all man's desires, could, it was said, be stimulated by public spending to offset the effect of an economic slump. Demand, political will allowing, could also be dampened down during economic booms should inflation get out of control.

Both demand management and ideas of the welfare theorists may seem impractical and idealistic to an ordinary manager. How, after all, can one reliably measure such subjective concepts as utility or national demand? Is it even reasonable, when the meaning of such measures may change, to plot historical trends?

Nevertheless welfare economics and demand management, help us understand the ideas that lay behind what might be called the welfare confidence of the 1950s, 1960s and early 1970s. The Beveridge Report of 1942, (Cmnd. 6404 – Report on Social Insurances and Allied Services) set the tone for confident welfare measures.

This report recommended free medical services, unemployment insurance, retirement pensions, child allowances, funeral allowances and generally inspired the National Assistance Act 1948. The so-called 'cradle to grave' Welfare State, which the aforementioned act ushered in, was perhaps the most obvious manifestation of a growing feeling of welfare confidence. The country had won (with the help of our allies) the greatest and most terrible war in history. Britain still had an empire. The government was powerful and in control in a 'Keynesian' way of the economy. Government experts – economists, social scientists, and managers – could, or should, be able to solve any problems, starting with poverty.

By the late 1970s in Britain and the US the so-called monetarists (who emphasized the importance of controlling the supply of money in circulation, basically as a measure of lowering inflation and interest rates) were gaining the upper hand over the Keynesians. Welfare confidence in terms of the increasing role of the public sector as a direct provider gave way in the face of 'stagflation' – rising inflation combined with rising unemployment and economic stagnation. Most readers will, no doubt, be familiar with the controversy and events of the 1980s and early 1990s, further comment on which will be left to posterity.

Such economic viewpoints – and there are a great many more – are useful in helping to understand the broad span of what has occurred, at least in western industrial democracies and as a backdrop against which the public sector manager might take his or her decisions. The manager will be likely to appreciate more fully his or her role if this role can be seen in its wider context. But beyond this the author does not propose to go. An appreciation of public sector origins and the rationale of its existence is useful and necessary but far less than sufficient for good auditing and good management decision-making.

Concluding points

We have considered very briefly some legal, moral, historical and economic insights into the public sector. The lack of choice underlying taxation imposes a special duty on public servants. Fraud and corruption take on a special significance in the public sector.

There is a long and constantly changing history of public sector bodies. But in a modern western society the public sector, however defined, seems bound to account for a sizeable proportion of GNP. This means that there will always be considerable public interest in the standards of public accountability and any suspicion of fraud and corruption will need to be positively refuted.

Although a continuing public sector appears inevitable, safeguards and internal controls sufficient to ensure full accountability, fairness and honest behaviour have to be deliberately sought and maintained. The remaining chapters of this book aim to show the reader how to seek out and maintain such practices and behaviour without encouraging the volume of red tape to increase out of control.

References

A good introduction to the economics of the public sector is provided by *Public Sector Economics* by C. V. Brown and P. M. Jackson, published by Basil Blackwell. Indicative of the works of writers mentioned in this chapter are the following.

1. Mumford, L. (1961). *The City in History: Its Origins, its transformations and prospects*. Secker and Warburg, London.

2. See Baird, A. M. (1971). 'Wagner's Law of Expanding State Activity' in *Public Finance*, **26**.

3. Rostow, W. W. (1971). *Politics and the Stages of Growth*. Cambridge University Press.

4. Peacock, A. T. and Wiseman, J. (1961). *The Growth of Public Expenditure in the UK*. Princeton University Press.

5. Pigou, A. C. (1928). *A Study in Public Finance*. Macmillan.

6. Keynes, J. M. See, for example, *How to Pay for the War*. Macmillan (1940) or the more famous work. *The General Theory of Employment, Interest, and Money*. Macmillan (1936).

3

Using systems-based auditing

Introduction

This is an appropriate point in the book to consider fraud and corruption from the perspective of the systems-based approach to audit. The systems-based approach to audit has been widely adopted largely because it highlights – for the benefit of both managers and auditors – key strengths and weaknesses in an organization's financial controls. Guarding against fraud and corruption should be borne in mind in any audit, though it is unlikely to be uppermost in the thoughts of an auditor undertaking say, 'attestation' or 'VFM' audits, unless circumstances change dramatically after the audit has been planned.

Since the early 1970s the systems-based approach, with subtle variations, has gone a long way towards supplanting the more traditional 'investigatory' or 'probity' approach to audit. Auditors who are particularly concerned with risk of fraud have sometimes viewed this development with concern. A traditional approach to fraud has been to respond to suspicions based on audit work or alleged cases. This would entail detailed investigation of individual transactions, files relating to decisions and any other evidence. At times the traditional approach may still be required, but the systems-based approach (SBA) offers certain definite advantages as follows:

1. It can highlight 'risky' areas of weak control that often go unsuspected in a traditional approach.
2. It can offer a more structured approach to planning and carrying out the audit. In particular SBA can point to areas where the probity/investigatory role should be concentrated.
3. It can offer systematic audit evidence on the totality of a system (rather than being limited to its individual parts) without the necessity to undertake detailed testing on all stages of transaction processing. Of course, the evidence may indicate that the system is unreliable in which case detailed testing will still be required if an opinion on the accuracy of the system output, e.g. a final balance sheet figure, is required.

Modern audit works devote considerable attention to the systems-based approach to audit and it is not our intention to reiterate this in detail.

For the benefit of the manager or any other professional who is unfamiliar with a systems-based audit, we present below a brief overview. This overview is split into five stages that, taken on their own, may tend to give too narrow and rigid an impression of the course of a typical audit. This simplification is unfortunate but, short of including several lengthy chapters devoted entirely to systems-based audit, it will have to suffice. Even this short summary should, it is hoped, be sufficient for the non-specialist reader to appreciate the important role of systems-based audits in helping to prevent fraud and corruption. The reader who requires more than a summary is recommended to choose at least one book from the general section of Further reading.

A summary of the systems-based approach to audit

The objectives of a systems-based audit will typically fall into categories (1) or (3) as described in Table 3.2.

Once objectives have been agreed, the detailed approach needs to be planned, the essence of which can be stated under five broad headings: Recording the system; Undertaking an initial evaluation; Undertaking compliance and substantive testing; Reviewing the work and Opinion forming and reporting.

Recording the system

To do this the auditor will need to be clear what he means by the 'system'. He will need to set boundaries, which may be quite arbitrary at times, to separate procedures that are related and designed to achieve a planned objective from those that are not. This is often not as difficult as it sounds. The audited organization usually has management-defined systems which correspond well to systems from an audit viewpoint. Purchases, debtors, creditors, payrolls are large main systems that usually form key parts of the financial structure of an organization. These and some others are given as examples below.

Purchases
Stock control
Creditors' payments
Debtors (sundry)
Payrolls
Capital expenditure
Loans
Investments
Cash collection
Fixed assets accounting
Means-tested benefits (housing benefits, social security, etc.)
General bookkeeping and accounts
Grant (income/expenditure)
Tax/income (revenue collection)

Most auditors record the system by diagrammatically 'flow-charting' the procedures and compiling system notes. (Detailed examples of flow-charting together with blank specimen papers, are given by Jones, P. and Bates, J. (1990) Public Sector Auditing, Chapman & Hall.) Completing an internal control questionnaire – a series of questions and answers designed to document the important control procedures – is also useful. At times simply copying and amending management's own procedural instructions, work manuals, etc. may be sufficient. Often what merits attention as a large main system in one organization may be of little consequence in another. The main source of income for many public sector bodies is from exchequer grants and the main cause of expenditure can be salaries and wages. Other bodies have a mixture of fees, grants, and taxes and may move funds about in complicated ways. The auditor must decide which systems merit attention and the precise cut-off (if any) between, say, purchases and creditors' payments – two systems that often overlap.

Whenever a systems-based audit is undertaken, sub-systems tend to become apparent. Debtors may arise from several billing sources; fees may be charged by different, sometimes relatively isolated, parts of the same organization. Stocks may be controlled from more than one storehouse or depot. Again, the auditor must define, using professional judgement and bearing in mind his own and management's objectives, the extent of the system or sub-system under audit.

Undertaking an initial evaluation of the system

Initial evaluation involves defining the system control objectives and isolating those procedures or relationships within the system that constitute controls from those that do not. These very important aspects usually make up most of the effort involved in any initial evaluation and are explained in detail later in the chapter. For the moment we shall consider some overview aspects of the initial evaluation that can easily be overlooked when the auditor is under pressure.

Overview aspects

Initial evaluation should consider the overall suitability and adequacy of the system to fulfil its basic role or objectives. Such a basic role is sometimes forgotten amongst the detail of procedures. For example, the auditor should check that creditors' payments are not merely a poorly organized adjunct of various devolved purchasing arrangements but are undertaken, usually centrally, in an organized and controlled environment. The auditor should consider too the financial information produced by the system and whether or not such a system is suitable for its intended output. Another example might be fixed assets which may be shown as 'depreciated' or simply retained at cost but supplemented by 'capital discharged' in the main accounting system. Is the system he is considering able, at least in principle, to comply with the statutory requirements and any internal regulatory provisions laid down? If such wider questions as these are not given attention before the bulk of the work is undertaken much effort may be wasted. Opportunities to see the wood despite the trees can easily be missed.

Detailed evaluation

Once such overview aspects have been considered the auditor sets about defining the 'control' objectives and identifying the key internal controls (from among all the procedures he has recorded) that help satisfy those 'control' objectives. There are some examples in Table 3.1. If the non-specialist reader has difficulties in appreciating their full significance the examples may be reconsidered after control objectives and key controls have been discussed later on in this chapter.

NB: these examples can present only a fraction of the possible internal controls. For a great many systems control objectives and descriptions of controls will have to be tailor made to suit the individual audit assignment. Identification of controls requires experience and judgement and usually looks easier than it actually is!

Table 3.1 Examples of control objectives and key controls to meet those objectives (Neither the listed objectives nor the possible controls are meant to be exhaustive)

System	Control objective	Possible key control
Sundry debtors	(1) All debts due are raised. (2) All debts raised are correctly calculated and coded to the correct amounts. (3) All debts raised are recovered or otherwise actioned as follows: (a) payment received; (b) debt cancelled/credit note issued; (c) debt written off. (4) All debts are recovered or otherwise actioned in reasonable time.	(1) Value of invoices raised is monitored continuously against debt generating activity. (1) Spot checks are carried out by management on all fee charging activities. (1) and (2) Outstanding debtors are 'circularized' by auditors. (2) Only officially checked and authorized invoices are used to collect debts. (3) Invoices are pre-numbered and payment is instructed to be made only to the organization's account. (1) to (4) A separation of duties exists between debt generating activity/debt accounting and management (including credit control)/ bank reconciliation. (3) and (4) Debtors control accounts and aging report are actioned by senior management. (2) and (4) All write-offs and cancellations are authorized by a senior manager without direct responsibility for the sundry debtors function. (3) and (4) All write-offs over a minimum value are reported to a committee of political members/appointees.
Sundry creditors	(1) Only bills made out to and due by the organization are paid. (2) All bills paid are for goods and services satisfactorily received or performed. (3) All goods and services received were genuinely requested by the organization.	In most sundry creditors systems some kind of payment authorization either accompanies all invoices to be paid or might even be stamped on the invoice. This usually performs a key control function and should include recognizable signatures certifying that: (3) the invoice has been matched to the appropriate order(s);

Table 3.1 (*contd*)

System	Control objective	Possible key control
	(4) All payments made are correctly calculated (including coding to correct account, taking into account any credit notes and discounts allowed).	(2) goods/services have been checked and found satisfactorily; (4) the calculations are correct. (1) to (4) A senior officer should sign to authorise payment, checking (1) and that responsible officials have agreed (2), (3) and (4). (2) Delivery advice notes are signed by storeman and a copy retained. (It may not be possible for a storeman to check all items delivered before the consignor's vehicle leaves the premises. If the storeman is forced to check the delivery sometime after it has taken place he should immediately annotate any discrepancy on the advice note and *not* sign any payment authorization until the supplier or consignor has agreed to the discrepancy.) (1) All invoices are stamped 'paid' after payment. This helps avoid deliberate or accidental duplicate payment.
Salaries system	(1) Salaries costs are incurred only for authorized employees. (2) All starters, leavers, promotion and similar major changes are correctly and promptly actioned. (3) All salaries costs are correctly calculated and coded.	(1) to (3) A separation of duties exists between the authorization of recruitment, promotion and similar changes – usually done by a personnel branch – and payroll input/accounting – usually the responsibility of an accounts branch (1) and (2) A reconciliation of authorized staff in post from personnel records to payroll is undertaken by independent officers, e.g. internal audit on an *ad hoc* basis. (2) and (3) A payroll supervisor checks and initials all major payroll entries, e.g. on starting, promotion, leaving or upon changes in pay rates, allowances, etc. (3) Minor changes, e.g. address or bank code, are initialled by the officer updating the payroll.

Table 3.1 *(contd)*

System	Control objective	Possible key control
Rent collection	(1)Rent debits are raised for all properties.	(1) The total rent roll is reconciled periodically to rent debtors figure and to the property 'terrier'.
	(2) All rents are correctly calculated and charged (including any arrears/ adjustments/allowances).	(1) Purchases and sales of properties are notified to the housing rent accountant upon exchange of contracts, or on completion if new-builds.
	(3) All rents are collected.	(1) and (3) All new lets are notified to a housing rents accountant upon receipt of signed leasing agreements.
	(4) All collections are brought fully to account.	(2) All rent reviews are authorized and notified to collectors and rent accountant.
		(3) and (4) All rent payments are receipted on official rent account cards.
		(3) and (4) All rent collections including overs/unders are balanced against collection sheets and signed by collector.
		(4) All collections are banked by office cashier after agreement and signature on bank paying-in slip.
		(1) to (4) A separation of duties exists between collections (collectors) rent accounting (accountant) banking (cashier) and, if possible, bank reconciliation (accountant).

Comprehensive examples of internal controls are available in CIPFA's ICQ Training Package and CIPFA's Internal Control Checklists, both available from the Institute.

Undertaking compliance and substantive testing

It is all very well for the auditor to identify internal controls but the most important question is: were the controls actually put into operation and maintained effectively throughout the period in question? To decide the answer to this the auditor must undertake compliance testing. *Compliance testing*, basically, seeks to check that control procedures which have been identified are in practice actually operated, and then to record the evidence of this operation for further audit work and evaluation. Evidence could be, for example, that:

1. authorizations were signed by the appropriate manager;
2. reconciliations balanced correctly;
3. a separation of duties was observed;
4. official pre-numbered receipts were given;
5. management checks were fully recorded.

If the auditor seeks assurance that the system actually managed to produce accurate and reliable figures or other output, substantive testing is an essential supplement to compliance testing. *Substantive testing* seeks to substantiate the accuracy, validity and completeness of assets, liabilities and transactions that occurred. In almost all audit assignments an element of substantive testing will be undertaken. After all, a system with inadequate control might still have performed well. Sometimes, in contrast, a system with very good controls that operated correctly and effectively for the whole audited period may have missed some unforeseen event. No system is perfectly designed. The amount of substantive testing will usually be determined by the results of compliance testing and the level of assurance the auditor wishes to offer the audited client.

The terms 'control' and 'test' objectives are sometimes found confusing. In fact they are virtually the same. It is important for the auditor to ensure that the control objectives that should have been satisfied by internal controls are still satisfied for each transaction tested substantively. When substantively testing the transactions the term 'test' objectives is often preferred. For example, a 'control' objective in a purchasing system may be that 'all purchases are genuinely required for the organization'. The auditor would usually check that controls exist to ensure all purchases are authorized by a senior officer and that any unusual items are likely to be questioned, perhaps by ensuring a separation of duties is maintained between

1. custody of the purchased goods;
2. authorization of purchases by a senior officer;
3. bookkeeping and recording by an accounts section.

If the auditor found, perhaps during compliance testing, that such controls were not operating in the purchases system, he or she would normally (after reporting the fact to management) proceed to undertake some level of substantive testing. The total level of testing would probably be greater than would have been envisaged at the start of the audit. For each purchase transaction the auditor would (among other things) still check it was genuinely required, i.e. valid, and therefore satisfied the objective outlined above. In this case the term 'test' objective is commonly used rather than 'control' objective.

Review stage

All the audit evidence should be reviewed from initial documentation through compliance testing to substantive testing. Audit and control objectives should be reconsidered in the light of the auditor's developing knowledge of the system. Any statements by management; replies from circulars or other enquiries sent to debtors and banks; any audit papers from other auditors; any analytical review work (a specialized form of substantive testing); and any other relevant evidence should be considered.

Review normally involves both interim review at convenient points as the audit progresses and a final review at the end of the audit. The final review should be done by experienced and senior staff, usually at management level.

Opinion forming and reporting

The auditor may well have been forming opinions throughout the audit and these should be annotated as interim conclusions or points for attention at the final review. The final overall opinion may be expressed briefly in a clear external audit certificate or it may be expressed at great length in a major internal audit report. In between these extremes lie various management letters, shorter audit reports, 'reports in the public interest' and so on.

The foregoing five stages are, not surprisingly, a gross over-simplification. A systems-based audit may be an end in itself or form part of wider audit with several systems-based assignments. Some audit work does not fall neatly and easily into the systems-based approach. The boundaries of the auditor's responsibilities are always changing and currently they are expanding into a wider consultancy-type role. Nevertheless this brief outline is essential for an understanding of the basic approach adopted by auditors.

An adapted systems-based approach to audit

For the rest of this chapter we seek to provide an adaptation of the basic systems-based approach designed to emphasize the aspects that will best guard against fraud and corruption. Much of what has already been said will be looked at afresh and from a more selective point of view.

It is important to stress that for more general audit objectives, particularly attestation audits, value for money audits and broad-based systems audits, this adapted approach would almost certainly be less than an adequate basis on which to form any professional opinions. The general auditor is far more concerned with 'innocent' errors (often repeated on a large scale), inaccurate or misleading disclosures of accounting information, waste and efficiency, or simply inadequate bookkeeping and management reporting. These wide-ranging concerns will rarely be satisfied simply by ensuring everything possible is being done to prevent fraud and corruption.

We must therefore be selective when dealing with fraud and corruption. Our selectivity starts by reconsidering our audit objectives and, in the light of these, designing a shorter and refined version of an internal control questionnaire (ICQ), using what are sometimes called 'key control' questions. The key control questionnaire (KCQ) leads the auditor into defining his or her control objectives, which should always be in line with the audit objectives. At some point, usually towards the end of the audit, it is very useful to compile a checklist. Each of the stages is outlined in the following paragraphs.

Audit objectives

The main types of audit objective are summarised in Table 3.2. Two of these are related primarily to fraud, 2 and 5, though the latter to its investigation rather than to its prevention. If we take the first of the fraud objectives and relate this to the two systems-based audit objectives 1 and 3 we see how the fraud objective is 'subsumed', so to speak, by the systems objectives.

A well-designed system will usually contain internal controls to safeguard the functioning and integrity of assets and enable it to process transactions validly, accurately and completely. By ensuring a sound system we are in effect ensuring that key controls exist to guard against fraud and corruption.

The foregoing high-level objectives have been chosen to exemplify the different types of audit undertaken. They are all no more than variants on a theme – forming professional opinions and expressing them in a report to the appropriate level of management. The precise wording of the audit objectives will, of course, need to be tailored to suit individual situations.

Table 3.2 Typical audit objectives

1. *System evaluation*
   To document the system, identifying and evaluating the internal controls and weaknesses.

2. *System evaluation in respect of fraud and corruption*
   To document the system identifying and evaluating those controls (and weaknesses) most likely to guard against (or contribute towards) risk of fraud and corruption.

3. *Full systems based audit*
   To form an opinion and report on the reliability of the internal controls operating in the system and the accuracy, completeness and validity of the financial information produced.

4. *Attestation (certification) audit*
   To form an opinion and report on the financial information (balance sheet, revenue account, management accounts, major contract final account, etc.) in accordance with statutory and/or professional certification requirements, e.g. 'true and fair', 'properly present', 'the final balance due', etc.

5. *Fraud investigation*
   To form an opinion on the validity of the accusation or suspicion of fraud, (corruption, misappropriation, etc.) reported by management or others or arising from the audit, and report on the appropriate further action to be taken by management.

6. *Value for money audit*
   To form an opinion and report on the economy/efficiency/effectiveness achieved by the audited function, department, body, etc.

7. To form an opinion and report upon the arrangements, including policies, corporate aims, information, internal controls and weaknesses, most likely to enhance or reduce value for money.

8. *Regulatory audit*
   To form an opinion on the organization's/department's/function's ability to comply with statutory and in-house regulations.

The term 'probity' audit is sometimes used to describe the detailed 'vouching' of individual transactions or investigation of an auditor's suspicions. Probity audit is subsumed under detailed substantive testing carried out under full systems-based audit, regulatory audit or when undertaking fraud investigation.

During a major audit assignment such as the attestation audit of a large set of financial accounts, or during two or three similar assignments, such as the systems-based audits of several related systems, numerous internal controls will be considered and usually a great deal of testing will be done. The fraud and corruption audit objectives will not, initially, be the primary objectives of the auditor. Later on, if the auditor becomes concerned with fraud and corruption he may well need to plough his way through a great many working papers and reports.

Much of this effort can be avoided, or at least shortened significantly, by introducing two stages as mentioned above: firstly the compilation of a key control questionnaire at the start of each audit; and secondly the compilation of a fraud and corruption checklist at the end of the audit when all the controls and weaknesses have been fully assessed.

Key control questions (KCQs)

The auditor's method is, basically, to stand back from the fine detail of the system and in the light of the audit objectives (see Table 3.2), to ask what could happen within the system to prevent him or her forming a favourable opinion.

The manager can adopt almost the same approach, though he is more directly concerned with the management objectives of the system: what can go so seriously wrong that the whole or a large part of the purpose of the system is negated?

Usually, though not always, the key question from both auditor's and management's approaches turn out to be the same. Not surprisingly both auditor and manager usually have quite similar objectives.

Financial systems rarely have more than a few main purposes. Normally these involve the payment of bills or receipts of income, or both. The guarding of valuable assets including the prevention of disclosure of confidential information, the maximization of benefits (e.g. investments) or minimization of losses are other examples. This is why the number of key control questions is usually only three or four, perhaps six at most. The method is best explained in detail by examples.

Example 1

This concerns a sundry creditors system, the basic objective of which is to pay creditors the correct amount, on time, (but which should have concern for proper authorization, trade discounts, the cash flow position of the organization and any other appropriate management objectives).

Can only properly invoiced bills be paid?   The general rule is: No invoice, no payment. The invoice must be proper to the organization, not, say, an employee's gas bill, and it must have gone through an acceptable set of authorizing procedures, including checking the calculation of the invoice and agreement, when appropriate, to supporting orders and other documents.

Are only goods and services that have been satisfactorily received or performed paid for?   This, again, assumes a reasonable payment authorizing procedure in which some senior officer takes responsibility for certifying satisfaction with the goods or services.

Can only goods or services that were genuinely required by the organization be received or performed? It is not unusual to observe sound controls over payment once, say, work has been done; but was it really necessary, and if so who authorized it? Similarly were all goods, even if they were received in perfect condition, actually ordered by an authorized officer who is confident they will be used in the near future? In recent years the number of 'false billing' agencies has increased. A service such as inclusion in a trade or international directory is usually selected by such agencies as one for which responsibility within an organization is often not immediately apparent. The assumption, often correct, is that one officer will think another has requested the service and no one will expect to be in possession of evidence of the service before making payment.

Is the organization billed for all goods and services properly received? At first the auditor or manager may be tempted to ignore this question. ('If our suppliers forget to bill us – tough! All the more for us!') But there are two serious concerns that this, sometimes a fairly common attitude, ignores. Firstly, any responsible organization, particularly in the public sector, has its reputation and good will to maintain, both of which can be greatly enhanced by complete honesty towards suppliers. Secondly, and of greater risk from an audit viewpoint, the lack of an invoice may indicate fraud and corruption within both the recipient and the supplying organizations, though collusion will be required to perpetuate such a fraud.

Experienced auditors will notice that the questions above are far fewer and more generalized than those that typically make up an internal control questionnaire or ICQ. Also, important key questions that relate primarily to the wider objectives of audit are missing. If we were to list similar 'non-fraud' type key questions such as: 'Are all payments timed to optimize trade credit and prompt payment discounts?' 'Are all payment amounts accurately and fairly disclosed in the published accounts?' then the selectivity aimed for would be lost.

The purpose of a KCQ is quite different from the more commonly used ICQ. An ICQ helps the auditors to document the system by indicating procedures in detail and what controls are present. The purpose of a KCQ, as we shall see, is to identify the control or test objectives of the audit. Two further examples of KCQs are given below in summary form.

Example 2

This concerns a payroll system where the following questions may be asked.

1. Can only genuine employees be paid?
2. Are all genuine employees paid the correct amounts?
3. Are all 'leavers' actioned?

Example 3

This concerns a debtors collection system. The questions here are the following.

1. Are all debts owed raised?
2. Are all debts raised owed?
3. Are all debts raised actioned, i.e. paid, cancelled or written off?
4. Are all debts, cancellations and write-offs, correctly calculated, coded and authorized?

Again, the detailed arrangements for credit control and doubtful debts commonly associated with a full audit of debtors systems are not covered in this approach for the same reasons of selectivity as noted with the creditors KCQ.

Control objectives and key controls

Key control questions are merely a useful first stage in formulating and expressing the control (or testing) objectives of the audit. KCQs can be reworded as key control objectives basically by expressing the questions as a statement. For the payroll system, Example 2, the KCQs can be expressed as the following key control objectives.

Objective	Related KCQ
(a) All employees are genuine, i.e. properly authorized.	1 and 3
(b) Only current employees are paid.	2
(c) Only due amounts are paid/deducted.	2 and 3
(d) All the amounts paid/deducted are correctly calculated.	2

Thus the ability to, say, bring about an unauthorized regrading would mean that objective (c) was not met by the controls in the system. Objectives (c) and (d) are similar but should not be confused – a control may ensure all amounts are correctly calculated but not check that they were actually due.

The audit assignment objectives already outlined in Table 3.2 are, in most audits, too broad to assist the auditor in directing his effort when identifying and compliance testing internal controls or carrying out substantive testing of individual transactions. The audit requires control objectives in line with the audit objectives. These should provide clear beacons toward which the auditor can direct his or her efforts. The control objectives help the auditor decide whether a procedure he has identified when documenting a system is simply one among many that are convenient for the processing activities to continue in an orderly manner, or whether the procedure is a key control. *Procedures without which one or more of the control objectives would be seriously impaired are key controls.*

In, for example, a wages system the allocation of a correct code for the paypoint may be required. If this is mis-allocated some payslips may be distributed to, say, the vehicles maintenance section rather than, say, the central accounts section. This would cause some initial inconvenience and no doubt some urgent telephone calls but in the end each employee will get his or her wages and the wages clerk will get a mild ticking-off. This procedure has no material effect on any control objectives listed above and it is not a key control.

However, if the incorrect pay code relates to a point on an incremental grading structure which results in the employee's receiving an on-going over-payment this would affect objective (c) of due payment. If, to take another example, procedures relating to the setting up of a new employee and the cancellation of a leaver are not subject to internal controls, then the risk of a 'ghost' employee is substantially increased, affecting the first control objective. Procedures and arrangements that prevent these errors are clearly, in these circumstances, key controls.

To summarize, we have adapted the systems-based approach concentrating on four stages:

1. defining audit objectives;
2. asking key control questions and selecting those relating to fraud and corruption;
3. formulating control objectives relating to fraud and corruption;
4. identifying controls to meet these objectives.

The fourth is an important stage in fraud work whether carried out as a routine preventative audit assignment, or as part of an investigation into what went wrong and how mistakes of the past can be avoided in the future.

If no effective controls are apparent, as is often the case in some smaller or poorly resourced systems, then the control objectives can be taken as test objectives and extensive substantive testing of transactions should be under-taken to achieve the test and thence the audit objectives.

If, as is normally to be expected, effectively designed controls are apparent then these should be compliance tested as part of the client's routine systems-based audit. During compliance testing the auditor tests the operation of the control rather than the detail of the transaction. Thus equal importance is attached to all errors, irrespective of the value of the items being tested. If £5 and £10 vouchers were not correctly authorized the auditor cannot assume that £5000 and £10 000 vouchers, processed in the same system and subject to the same controls, were correctly authorized.

Interpreting the results of compliance testing calls for skill and judgement. This point is of such importance it is worth repeating: the results of compliance testing will help determine the level of substantive testing to be undertaken. A system may, on initial evaluation and documentation, appear to have adequate internal control. But upon completion of compliance testing it may be found that the controls that were initially documented are, in practice, ignored or ineffective. Thus the ultimate effect of compliance testing is to determine the level of substantive testing. Management must be informed of any lack of effective control but only by substantive testing will the auditor know whether or not such lack of control resulted in any fraud or errors in the information produced by the system and used by management for taking important decisions. This is also a particularly important point for the external auditor who verifies information in the accounts. His professional reputation may be called into question if his opinion was based upon inadequate testing.

Fraud and corruption checklists

These are usually no more than extractions of 'fraud and corruption tests' from the wider body of compliance and substantive testing that usually form the bulk of routine systems-based audits. They serve two main purposes.

1. To bring together at the end of one or more audit assignments all those tests that will show the work done to guard against fraud and corruption. This is particularly useful if the risk of malpractice is considered relatively high. Such tests are usually the ones that enable the auditor to be sure he has satisfied an important part of his audit objective(s).
2. Periodically, as part of his usual professional practice, the auditor will need to review and be sure he is carrying out adequate work designed specifically to guard against fraud and corruption. If such checklists are prepared for each main client body, department or function, as appropriate, such review is made much simpler and more effective. This is particularly important for auditors with statutory responsibilities.

Summary

This chapter has introduced the reader to some basic audit approaches and suggested ways in which these can be fine-tuned to the requirements of preventing fraud and corruption. If some auditors find the chapter rather too basic they are reminded that the approach – documentary systems, asking key control questions, identifying controls and compliance and substantive testing – is not solely the prerogative of the auditor. Certainly the stages prior to testing are suitable for any manager or other professional concerned to minimize risk of malpractice.

The approach is, at the start, akin to a general manager setting out his or her business objectives, then asking what effect if any the presence or absence of a particular procedure will have on achieving these objectives. Those concerned to form a professional audit opinion must then go on to undertake testing. This applies as much to opinions on the effectiveness of measures to guard against fraud and corruption as to opinions on the fairness of a balance sheet.

Case studies

The following case studies are chosen to illustrate situations in typical systems-based audits.

Case study 3.1 Stores issues audit

This case study is taken from a very basic audit assignment. The study selects some of the working papers to show the audit objective and how key control questions relate to the control objectives of the audit. This is followed by explanatory notes of the main control risks. The reader should bear in mind that the working papers are taken out of the context of the whole audit and for this reason no conclusions can be made on the adequacy or otherwise of the audit work in satisfying the audit objectives. No detailed findings, conclusions or recommendations are given at this stage.

In this case, for ease of illustration, we have defined the stores issuing system relatively narrowly. We have not, for example, asked as a key control question: 'Are all authorized issues used for the intended purpose?' We have assumed that the stores is a central system serving many user systems and that this question will apply to the audit of each user system.

At first sight several useful controls appear to exist in this system, but on further examination these are not well designed and other important controls that might be expected are missing.

Contents of case study

Internal Audit KCQ
Working paper – Audit assignment summary
Working paper – Interview notes
Working paper – Procedure notes
Stocks issuing system – Notes on controls and weaknesses
Other considerations

ENCL REF I1
FILE REF AUD 11.B

Internal audit KCQ

PREPARED BY AB DATE 28. 1. X2
REVIEWED BY __ DATE _____

Assignment: Stocks and stores issues

Key control questions are as follows.

Are all authorized issues genuinely required? In answer to this question the auditor would need to examine the requisitioning procedure. Ideally a responsible officer could certify that the goods are required for a defined job or other clear reason. Only a limited number of senior officers would, normally, be authorized to make out requisitions for laid-down values or a range of goods related to their rank and responsibilities. Copies of requisitions should be retained, be subject to occasional selected checking by management and be readily available for audit.

Can only authorized issues be made? Here the auditor will need to examine the procedure of actually issuing stocks, the physical security of the stocks, the nature of the issue notes and what, if any, checks are available to ensure completeness and accuracy of issue.

These key control questions help the auditor to formulate the internal control objectives as shown on the first working paper.

Internal audit – working paper

PREPARED BY AB DATE 20. 1. X2
REVIEWED BY   DATE

Assignment:	Stocks and stores issues

AUDIT ASSIGNMENT SUMMARY

Audit objective: To document and evaluate internal controls and weaknesses in the stock issuing system.

Control objectives: To ensure:
  – All issues are genuinely required.
  – All issues are promptly authorized.
  – All issues are completely and accurately recorded.

Audit approach: – Last audit's working papers are to be reviewed and amended as appropriate.
  – Main stores held at the depot and other stock-holding sites of a material size are to be visited.
  – Stores staff to be interviewed to ascertain/confirm main procedures.
  – Internal controls and weaknesses to be identified.
  – Compliance and substantive test programmes to be made up or revised, and undertaken as appropriate.
  – Form opinion and draft report for chief internal auditor to revise.
  – Chief internal auditor to report, as appropriate, to chief officer responsible for stores.

Internal audit – working paper

PREPARED BY AB DATE 1. 2. X2
REVIEWED BY   DATE

Assignment:	Stocks and stores issues
	INTERVIEW NOTES
Storekeeper:	No change in procedures since last audit but the introduction of fuel 'charge cards' for use at selected local garages has been suggested by management and is currently under consideration.
Senior storekeeper:	Year-end stocktake was due to be carried out and senior storekeeper was engaged in preparation. Interview had to be limited to approximately ten minutes rather than the half hour or so intended. The senior storekeeper was unable to produce a list with specimens of current signatures of officers authorized to sign requisitions.
DSO manager:	To date, nearly all outside purchase of these stocks have been delivered to the depot. 'Direct to site' deliveries are due to start for a wide range of building materials in approximately two days time.

ENCL REF M18
FILE REF AUDS 11.B

Internal audit – working paper

PREPARED BY AB DATE 2. 2. X2
REVIEWED BY   DATE

Assignment: Stocks and stores issues

PROCEDURE NOTES

Main stores – Building and other works Issues to employees are only made on authority of a signed job–requisition slip, made out and signed by site supervisor or by DSO manager/assistant manager. Requisitions are not pre-numbered but are retained by the storekeeper in date order for up to one year.

Any issue for goods valued at over £1000 should, according to financial regulations, be countersigned by the senior engineer client side. No countersigned requisitions have come to light in the last June 1988 audit or the one before that, May 1986.

Main stores – transport vehicles, fuel and parts As for building works; except that vehicles (identified by registration mark) are recorded on the 'route log' and signed out by fleet manager on a daily basis. Drivers are issued with vehicle requisition slips which must have 'start' and 'finish' mileages recorded and initialled by the driver.

Stocks issuing system notes

The following notes identify the controls, of which there are relatively few in this case, and the main weaknesses. The auditor would normally annotate these points, briefly, on a summary or alongside the relevant part of the flowchart. Here they are discussed in more detail to highlight the severe risks involved.

Note 1

> *'Issues to employees are only made on the authority of a signed job requisition slip, made out and signed by a site supervisor or by DSO manager/assistant manager...'*

Essentially this is, or should be, an important control to ensure proper authorization. Nothing is issued unless one of a limited number of senior officers authorizes the issue. It could however be significantly improved if the slip was made out and initialled by the employee who wishes to use the items to be issued and is then signed by the senior officer. Apart from initialling the slip this is what is likely to happen in any case so, for little if any extra cost, the control is enhanced by reducing the risk of collusion and requiring two people to accept responsibility for the issue of an item. If the slip was later questioned the chance of at least one person being found to give a satisfactory answer is increased.

The risks of a 'forged' issue are also reduced as an authorized signature and an employee's initials would have to be forged. This is particularly important as the senior storekeeper mentioned appears to have no up-to-date list of authorized signatures and there appears to be no evidence that the senior storekeeper or anyone else checks that the signatures appear genuine.

Note 2

> *'Requisitions are not pre-numbered but are retained by the storekeeper, in date order, for up to one year.'*

Pre-numbering is a useful control to ensure all issues are recorded as it enables any missing forms to be highlighted. Ideally copies should be filed in number order with a signed explanation of any gaps, e.g. 'specimen taken for audit purposes'.
One year is hardly likely to be sufficient time for legal or audit purposes.
Various risks occur due to lack of pre-numbering. If the auditor or a manager felt any issue was unreasonable, for example on a site visit to construction works, the storekeeper (or anyone else) could simply remove

all evidence of an issue by destroying the issue requisition. In any case of corruption, or simply poor control over ordering/usage of materials, blame would be difficult to apportion.

Note 3

> *'Any issue for goods valued at over £1000 should, according to financial regulations, be countersigned by the senior engineer...'*

This is typical of the kind of procedure which ideally might add an element of internal control to ensure issues are genuinely required, but in practice is virtually impossible to enforce. It has probably been included in financial regulations along with the more useful and practical requirement that all purchases over £1000 should be countersigned by a senior engineer. Given that in this case the engineer is on the client side, the DSO (a contractor) is unlikely to want to be charged with the cost or face any delay associated with this regulation.

The need for countersigning exceptionally large or valuable issues may well be genuine, in which case it should be undertaken by, say, a DSO manager. However, the value of the issue (unlike purchases) is often difficult to estimate (FIFO? LIFO? AVCO?) and it is usually far more realistic to stipulate that issues of materials of named valuable categories or over stipulated quantities should be countersigned.

Note 4

> *'Interview had to be limited...'*

The reasons for this may be genuine but concerns arise because, if notice was given of the visit as seems implied, the senior storekeeper may be simply evading the auditor. Also, as a general rule, storekeepers should not be directly involved in year-end stocktakes and the auditor should be concerned for the nature of the 'preparation' if this appears to be taking up much time.

Other considerations

Are the requisition slips crossed off after the last entry and before authorization? This control helps meet all three control objectives, mainly as it prevents extra items being added to authorized slips.

It seems that only one copy of an issue requisition is made out. At least two copies are required (one for the requisitioning/authorizing officer and one for the senior storekeeper) to maintain a reasonable control.

Whatever improper alterations or destruction occur to the active copy held by the senior storekeeper the passive copy could be used to detect these unless collusion is widespread.

The vehicle requisition slips offer slightly better control but still suffer from many of the above weaknesses. No procedures are apparent for logging vehicles back into the depot at night. Are drivers allowed to keep them at home? If so does anyone check that private mileages are not unreasonable?

Vehicle fleet management is a complex area particularly with regard to mileage and fuel costs. In view of imminent introduction of 'charge cards' a great many risks/problems need attention. Direct to site deliveries also involve risks and some very basic questions need further consideration, e.g.

- Does anyone have overall responsibility for route-scheduling and keeping mileages to a minimum?
- Can the cards be used at any time and for any vehicle or only for vehicles/drivers identified on the card?
- Schemes can provide valuable monitoring information for management. Is any management information (other than bills) provided by this scheme?
- Who has authorized the fairly major changes involving charge cards and direct-to-site deliveries?
- Has any cost benefit analysis or other detailed evaluation of these changes been undertaken?

The direct-to-site deliveries are usually more risk-prone than deliveries to a controlled point such as the depot. (See Chapter 6, the section on purchasing, for further details.)

Case study 3.2 Checking for ghosts

Payroll 'ghosts' are a well-known type of fraud. Yet they continue to occur despite all the warning signs. Managers, it seems, have to keep on relearning all the old lessons. The following case study outlines a pessimistic scenario in an attempt to emphasize the variety of possible ways these ghosts can appear.

This case assumes the auditor has come to the end of the full systems-based audit. The main parts of his report relating to his approach and detailed findings are considered, showing the control objectives and the inadequacy of internal controls. The case then goes on to discuss the ghost check implemented in response to these very disturbing findings. The ghost check reveals several payroll ghosts and the case discusses how these arose and what detailed precautions should have been taken. The main counter-measures are underlined and a summary of causes is given at the end of the case.

The Warranty Assessment Commissioning Office (WACO) is a major agency of a (fictional) central government department. It employs 3000 civil servants, 1500 at WACO HQ and 1500 at approximately 50 local offices. All officers are monthly paid salaried employees. During holiday periods temporary staff, often students, are taken on.

The chief internal auditor of WACO has received the following, rather disturbing, draft report from one of his auditors.

CONFIDENTIAL REPORT TO DIRECTOR OF WACO
FROM CHIEF INTERNAL AUDITOR

<u>PAYROLL AUDIT 19 X 2</u>

CONTENTS

Reference AB/LG 4007

Date

* Not included in the case study.

1. Introduction

This audit forms part of our agreed five-year audit strategy. The last major payroll audit took place almost exactly three years ago: Ref. DC/70301 dated 2.3. X9. At that time our findings were generally reassuring and all our recommendations were agreed. Since 2.3. X9 several interim audits have been undertaken and these are listed at Appendix 3.

3. Audit objective

To form an opinion on the reliability of the internal controls operating over the payroll system, and the accuracy, completeness and validity of the payroll information produced.

4. Audit approach

A full systems-based audit was undertaken. Officers were interviewed as per Appendix 1 and amendments were made to existing systems documentation, see Appendix 2. Internal controls were indentified on the basis of control objectives to ensure that:

(a) all employees are genuine;
(b) only genuine employees are paid;
(c) the amounts paid or deducted are due and correctly calculated.

The controls identified were compliance tested and a sample of the transactions processed were subjected to substantive testing. In this audit the control objectives were not met for the reasons discussed below.

5. Detailed findings:

5.1 The authorization and input to the computerized payroll (on-line and batch) is undertaken at WACO, although the mainframe computer is shared with several other government offices and is located at London. All output is received via screen, printout hard copy, or secure-courier tapes from which the pay-advice slips are printed. Salaries are paid directly by bank transfer into the payee's bank or building society account.

5.2 Appendix 2 shows an outline of the system, including a flowchart on which are listed the key controls and weaknesses.

5.3   Several key controls that were operational during our last audit are no longer so. The main cause of this appears to be the partial introduction of on-line terminal links to the mainframe computer centre that processes the payrolls. Just over one year ago the first stage in the replacement of batch processing with on-line terminals was completed. Due to several technical difficulties and inaccurate budget forecasting the second stage, which was due to be completed by next month, has only just started. The third and final stage has been put back until the latter half of next year.

5.4   This means that there are three separate categories of payroll processing currently operating at WACO; on-line, batch processing, and partial on-line processing. All payroll processing is also subject to some common procedures and controls irrespective of which category is chosen.

5.5   The staff involved in payroll processing have in many cases changed from our last visit. The general feeling of malaise and confusion generated by the failure to implement changes quickly and effectively is in stark contrast to our former impressions.

5.6   Management's attention should be drawn to the serious weaknesses in internal control identified during our initial evaluation and testing. Additional substantive testing is being undertaken in view of these findings and this may lead to further communications over the coming months.

5.7   Main area of weakness in internal control

5.7.1   Insufficient separation of duties Several examples were noted of temporary staff having been employed without implementing the usual recruitment procedures involving the personnel department. Examples were also noted of payroll officers with complete responsibility under the on-line system for inputting starters, changes, leavers, etc. and confirming the accuracy of the consequent output, including salary advice slips. In general, management seemed aware of these breakdowns in separation of duties, and excused them by the need to speed up procedures to deal with the growing backlog of work.

5.7.2   Inadequate input validation checks The new software for on-line processing omits any headcount comparison – of staffing levels authorized per division or section – to staff paid per division or section.

Under the old batch system of processing this was done automatically prior to production of a payroll. It is also noticeable that no upper-limit checks are performed on individual payments.

5.7.3   Lack of clearly defined responsibilities (audit trail) Apart from the usual difficulties in maintaining an audit trail through the computer, the trail of responsibility for authorizing and processing changes was not always apparent in the 'manual' parts of the system. Although most key documents contained sections for the initials or signatures of the officers responsible for calculating, entering dates, or authorizing changes these were seldom completed by payroll processing sections. Copies of the forms going forward for batch processing were rarely, if ever, sent back to the line division manager or section heads for confirmation that their requirements were being met. This was particularly noticeable in respect of the frequent overtime or 'substitution' duties where it is reasonable to assume that any overpayments to staff would probably remain unnotified.

5.7.4   Poor control over key documents Key documents used to input changes, were not prenumbered. These documents could easily have been obtained and completed by any one of nearly 100 officers including some with no direct payroll duties. Ideally these documents should be subject to the usual 'secure stationery' controls including stock control sheets with initials of officers issuing and receiving stock. Some key documents were very badly designed, particularly time sheets on which overtime payments were based. These documents contained space for far more entries than were ever likely to be made and none of those examined had been ruled-off prior to or during authorization. Several entries were made in different ink and may well have been written in after signed authorization had been given.

5.7.5   Lack of direct supervision and management information In all but one case, team leaders were expected to supervise 8–10 team members without any ability to observe directly the operations carried out. Team leaders were unable to review the documents processed by team members and were in effect no more than team advisers pre-occupied with attending to difficult queries from line departments or from the team members themselves. No attempt to monitor work in terms of volume, overtime, or allocation of payroll changes was under-taken, and no attempts to review the changes input by team members were apparent. Management information regarding transaction proces-sing time, volume, or allocated workloads, etc. was almost completely lacking. The management checks previously performed and recorded (evidenced during our last visit) seemed to have gradually lapsed over the past year to the point where they are no longer undertaken.

Commentary on the report and action taken

The conclusions and recommendations of this audit report go on to outline the rather obvious improvements required to 5.7.1 to 5.7.5 above. To illustrate how 5.7.1 to 5.7.5 above may be involved in cases of payroll ghosts we shall assume that the chief internal auditor, by now seriously worried about the integrity and accuracy of the payroll, decides to supplement the increased level of substantive testing with a full reconciliation of authorized staff in post to payroll – a so-called ghost check.

This is often not so difficult as it sounds, though it can be rather tedious for the auditor actually performing the reconciliation. Allowing for any peculiarities of organizational structure the following basic steps will usually be undertaken.

1. Choose, say, a recent payroll (any payroll may be chosen but the most recent is usually easiest).
2. Divide into departments (this is usually already done).
3. Obtain staff-in-post listings from personnel department or individual departmental managers as appropriate.
4. Deduct from 3 any of the chosen month's and subsequent month's starters who could not have been included in the chosen month's payroll. For starters during the chosen month it will be necessary to know the precise date of starting. A computerized payroll will probably require some days' advance notice for a starter's pay to be calculated and included in that month's pay run.
5. Add to 3 any officers who were officially classed as having left the organization but who were owed money during the month chosen.

It is usually quite difficult to obtain full details of all leavers who are still owed money. Arrears of pay may be discovered several months after an employee has left. The auditor will probably be left with a number of discrepancies relating to payments to former employees, each of which must be investigated. This is one important reason to pick a recent payroll. Also, staff, especially temporary staff recently laid off, may be retained on a payroll and a payment advice – but no cheque – produced each month in anticipation of their re-employment a few months later on.

At this point it should be possible to start reconciling staff in post to payroll. In most organizations the above information will be classified departmentally and it may be easier to take each main department at a time. In this case however inter-departmental transfers of staff will need to be identified to avoid double counting. Such an exercise could take several days in a medium-sized government department or local authority depending upon the number of queries.

The ghost check is only reliable when independent and accurate listings of staff-in-post are available. If all listings are prepared by the personnel officer, then any collusion between this officer and the payroll section could invalidate the above steps. If such collusion is suspected it should be possible to perform the ghost check provided that prime documents authorizing staffing levels have been agreed by senior management or political members. In extreme cases of collusion every authorized job description may need to be examined.

Assume that for this case a reliable staff-in-post listing was readily available and that the following ghosts came to light.

A.   Realscam

In this, possibly the worst case, one of the payroll team members was able to set up a completely fictitious employee.

A temporary employee, for which only a brief, forged, note from the line department is required on the pay file, was set up. No signature was required on the note and given the accepted lack of separation of duties between personnel and payroll functions no other clerk would be likely to question Realscam's origins. The team member had complete control over input and any changes to the pay details of Mr. Realscam. It was a simple matter to open a fictitious bank account in the required name. The lack of supervision and management checks meant that the file created was unlikely to be queried from above. Even if another team member input a routine change to Realscam's pay whilst the perpetrator was, say, on sick leave nothing suspicious would have been apparent. No audit trail of responsibility existed, so when Realscam was revealed by the ghost check the perpetrator(s) could not be identified. Several team members recalled Realscam but no one had any obvious reason in the circumstances to doubt his authenticity.

K. E. E. Pongoing

This was possibly the simplest case to arise. Mr. Pongoing was laid off but was not taken off the payroll. Originally this was an oversight, but the clerk who distributed the pay slips took advantage of the situation.

After several months had elapsed without Mr Pongoing notifying WACO of the continuing salary payments into his bank account he was paid a visit by the clerk. Pongoing, who was unemployed, receiving disability allowance and other welfare payments, had by this time spent most of the erroneous salary payments. During a subsequent court hearing he claimed that he had offered to repay what had by then amounted to several thousand pounds, in monthly instalments but had been told by the dishonest clerk that he had to repay the entire amount within 48 hours.

Pongoing panicked and offered a small bribe for the clerk to delay payment. Pongoing was easily intimidated by the clerk. Within a few more months he was to pay over to the clerk in cash almost the whole of each month's salary. The court found that most of the blame lay with the clerk who had misinformed and intimidated the relatively vulnerable and gullible Pongoing.

Adequate supervision or selective testing and regular use of management information on payroll changes would almost certainly have detected or more likely deterred this case. Ideally, of course, payroll slips should not be distributed by one clerk on a continuous basis.

R. E. Turn

Mrs Turn had been one of the regular 'temps' with a long history of periodic employment, who was known to have recently left the area. It was not unusual for salary advice slips to be posted to temporary employees who may only work for a few weeks at a time.

A messenger whose duties involved regular visits to the payroll section obtained several loose copies of change authorization forms. The temporary employees were amongst those still subject to batch processing and it was a simple matter to reactivate Mrs Turn with the dishonest employee's address. He had often seen the forms left casually on desks and in files in various stages of completion and it was not difficult to work out how to fill in the correct boxes. No signature needed to be forged, though even if one had, his ready access to completed forms would probably have enabled him to do that too. Once he was satisfied he had completed the forms correctly, all that was required was for it to be slipped into a batch waiting to be keyed in. At this point, very strong batch controls might have detected the crime. But in WACO as in most organizations, if the batch total actually keyed in differs from the expected or recorded totals on the batch header slip it is assumed that an innocent error has occurred. The batch now containing the forged input, was checked and the header slip amended. Inadequate input validation ensured no chance existed for the crime to be spotted on processing. Even relatively good validation checking may go no further than reasonableness checks over amounts and check digits, and it is unlikely to reveal anything worse than normal errors.

Once he had set up Mrs Turn the messenger stole more forms to authorize her temporary lay-offs and re-employments. Eventually the processed forms were returned to the payroll section, but as often happens with low priority filing, they were left unfiled for several days. Management said that the filing was delayed due to the backlog of work. In any event, there was plenty of opportunity for the false processed forms to be spirited away by the messenger.

So successful had his fraud become that the messenger had expanded his activities. By the time the ghost check brought them to light, the contents of his locker were found to resemble the payroll stationery cupboard. Three false temps and a full-time civil servant had been ghosted on to the payroll and all were recorded as residing at the messenger's address. The full-time civil servant had started off in the same way as the temps, but had been falsely promoted. This required a forged authorization signature on the false input form and in all probability would have led the messenger into more and more forged documents.

Given the general lack of control the auditors involved were of the opinion that this messenger could probably have continued his crimes undiscovered for some considerable time, though probably not indefinitely, had not the ghost check revealed them.

The most effective deterrent to Mrs Turn and her false colleagues is adequate control over stationery: all input forms authorizing starters, leavers and changes should be prenumbered and a simple stock register of all issues and the receiving officers kept. For example:

Date	From	To	No.	Held By	Signature	Balance
1.1.x1	1F 1000	10099	100	J. Bloggs	*J.Bloggs*	9,999

Any spoils, cancellations, etc. should be recorded by the officer responsible for holding the forms, which should be filled or ticked-off in numerical order upon return after processing.

It is often a remarkable fact that although organizations go to great length to safeguard, say, cash and leave a trail of responsibility for its handling, routine documents that can give rise to far greater losses are subject to quite inadequate controls.

The above examples of payroll ghosts could be enlarged by experienced auditors; those chosen illustrate how a systems-based audit

Table 3.3 Summary of possible cases of ghosts

The complete ghost
The lack of either adequate separation of duties or close supervision combined with complete autonomy over inputting major changes enabled Mr Realscam to be perpetrated. Even a completely false file existed on Realscam which though it may still have been compiled by a determined fraudster was made easier by the inadequate control of key forms.

Delayed termination
These cases like Mr Pongoing, are almost self-explanatory and are probably one of the most common cases of ghosts, especially when former employees are likely to be re-employed.

Back from the dead
This Mrs Turn type of case usually requires more nerve on the part of the perpetrator. Although it is similar in many ways to delayed termination, it can hardly be made to appear accidental.

The partial ghost
These are variants on the above but a genuine payee exists. Usually the genuine payee is given a false promotion or special allowance, is laid off a few days late, or there is a similar partial enhancement of payment. Often an error can occur which leads a payee or payroll clerk – or both in collusion – to perpetrate the false payments.

The on-off ghost
This type relies on frequent changing demand for labour. Again, like the partial ghost it may occur by accident. But to be perpetuated on a significant scale or for more than a few payments at least one party must behave dishonestly.

can reveal the likelihood or risk of fraud and corruption, even though no cases have come to light. A summary of some of these cases and some other plausible cases, brought to the author's attention at various times, is given in Table 3.3.

The parts of the detailed report not shown in this case explain to management how the audit and control objectives relate to maintaining a secure system and achieving the laid-down management objectives. These parts of the report are heavily dependent upon the nature and specific objectives of the organization and go far beyond our concern for preventing fraud and corruption. For these reasons, and to maintain anonymity, the full report is not outlined in this case study. The measures underlined in the above cases largely correspond to the conclusions and recommendations of the report.

Case study 3.3 Riscashire County Council

This case illustrates how a fraud and corruption checklist might be compiled, from audits undertaken throughout an organization. The checklist might be compiled at the audit planning stage to ensure that all areas thought potentially at risk are covered. But it is more usually compiled at the end of an audit, at the review stage, to give an overview of the total risk of fraud and corruption.

The external audit manager has embarked upon his final review of the $19 \times 3/4$ audit of this authority. One of the overall responsibilities is to review every three years the measures and controls to guard against fraud.

His approach is to review all the audit programmes currently in use, including this year's amendments, selecting tests that are of particular relevance in guarding against fraud and corruption. He will need to assess the results of these tests separately from the rest of his testing. This is because his testing is designed largely to give assurance on the accuracy of balance sheet and revenue account figures in order to satisfy his overall audit objective which will be worded in a similar way to 4, Table 3.2. He uses his best judgement to rank each test result as per Table 3.4 with a 'score' depending upon the frequency and significance of substantive and compliance errors.

He scores the risk as 0 for no errors, 1 if the acceptable level is reached for compliance or substantive testing; 2 if acceptable level is reached for both compliance and substantive testing; 3 if beyond acceptable level is reached for either type of testing, and so on up to 6.

In addition to reviewing the audit programmes, the auditor also reviews any known areas of fraud or high risk from his previous years' work and investigations and reports related to fraud.

It is not feasible to reproduce all the accumulated audit programmes that might be used on an external audit for a major local authority. An indication of the number and detail of such programmes is given by the Audit Approach section of the Audit Commission Auditor, published by

Table 3.4

	Score	Compliance errors	Substantive errors
High risk	6 5	Errors that indicate the control tested did not operate throughout the period	Errors that contribute to breaching materiality for this account and likely to be recurring
Beyond acceptable level	4 3	Errors indicate control did not operate for a substantial period or over a substantial volume of items	Numerous or high value errors or errors likely to be recurring
Acceptable Level	2 1	Very few errors that have affected only a few isolated low-value items	Very few errors of low value and unlikely to be recurring
Low risk	0	Nil errors	Nil errors

the Audit Commission for Local and Health Authorities in England and Wales. In practice many audit programmes and adaptations may be devised by individual firms or district auditors, to suit the needs of particular authorities. The following examples have been chosen merely to illustrate the methods described above – see Table 3.5.

One could continue thinking of examples of internal controls and compliance tests, especially in relation to capital works where procedures are usually both complex and tailored to meet the specific needs of each authority. To keep this case manageable the reader is asked to accept the above test as being adequate for Riscashire's circumstances.

For his checklist the auditor selects the following tests as particularly relevant in Riscashire's case in guarding against fraud and corruption: 2 to 5, 7 to 14, and 19.

In fact all the tests in this programme, may, in certain circumstances, be relevant in helping to prevent fraud and corruption. Capital contracts are notoriously prone to fraud and the audit programme will almost inevitably include a large proportion of key tests designed to cover fraud and corruption. Those selected above have been chosen on their general applicability rather than the 'but what if' scenario of any particular fraud.

The next audit programme has been chosen to illustrate a case where relatively few tests relate to fraud and corruption. Unlike capital works contracts it is usually the case that few tests relating to tree planting grants are designed primarily to guard against fraud and corruption and the auditor must be careful not to miss any that are relevant – see Table 3.6.

The auditor selects 1, 3, 7 and 8 for inclusion in his checklist. Although all of the above tasks might help prevent a particular instance of fraud or corruption, only 3, 7 and 8 have significant general applicability in this respect. Most of the other tests relate to detailed statutory or arithmetical checks which, given the small value of any one claim, are unlikely to reveal serious errors in total.

The importance of 3 and 7 is that for a fraudulent claim(s) to be processed three individuals would need to collude – the applicant and the two reporting officers. This level of collusion, though possible, is generally considered unlikely due to the scale of corruption required. Certainly if such collusion occurred it is difficult to see how any system could prevent fraud.

The majority of systems are likely to fall somewhere between the two programmes outlined above.

Let us assume that in this case the auditor has examined the main systems for Riscashire and selected compliance and substantive tests judged to be particularly relevant to his checklist.

He has reviewed the results of testing for each test and uses a method of scoring along the lines suggested in Table 3.4. Setting out his results in

Table 3.5 Compliance test programme capital works contracts

Prepared by: .... Reviewed: .... Encl. Ref: ....
Date: .... Date: .... File Ref: ....
Objective: To determine whether or not the internal controls identified in our systems documentation and evaluation (File x-3–4) have operated effectively throughout the period .... to ....

Control objectives	Control reference (see Flow chart)*	Test	Comments and cross reference to working papers
All contracts were necessary	Page 1 Point 3	1. Ensure each contract file has a feasibility and cost/benefit report if contract value exceeded £100 000. 2. For all contracts over £100 000 and a judgemental selection of those under that amount ensure there was a full report to the relevant committee who recommended implementation.	
All contracts were adequately authorized	Page 1 Point 6	As test 2 above; 3. Each page of contract general conditions and detailed specifications is signed by chief executive and chairman of the relevant committee after detailed scrutiny by senior architect/engineer/quantity surveyor as appropriate.	
	Page 1 Points 7 and 8	4. All variations to contract must be examined and agreed by architect/engineer/quantity surveyor as appropriate who must sign a variation order. All variations over £5000 or 5% of contract value must be approved by the relevant committee.	
All contracts were let on a fair basis between contractors invited to tender	Page 2 Point 10	5. Procedures for inviting tenders are vetted for compliance with standing orders by internal audit who compile working papers on each. (Standing orders relating to contracts are already designed to encourage fair letting of contracts.)	
	Point 12	6. All select lists of contractors are approved by the relevant committee.	

Table 3.5 *(contd)*

Control objectives	Control reference (see Flow chart)*	Test	Comments and cross reference to working papers
	Point 14	7. At least 25% of firms on select list must be invited for each contract. Each firm must be invited to tender for at least 25% of contracts.	
	Point 16	8. Identical tender conditions and specifications are given on the same day to all firms invited to tender.	
	Page 3 Point 18	9. All tenders received are logged upon receipt by the 'post clerk'.	
	Point 21	10. All tenders received are opened at the same time by chairman of committee, clerk, chief architect/engineer and one other member or senior officer and a schedule of tender sums is prepared by the clerk and signed by all of the above.	
	Points 22/23	11. If the lowest tender is not accepted the reasons must be set down in a report to the relevant committee.	
	Point 25	12. The schedule and report at 10 and 11 are reported, in summary, in the public minutes of the relevant committee.	
All contract work conformed to contract conditions		As per 4 above;	
	Point 27	13. Each stage payment is checked and certified by a quantity surveyor.	
	Point 29	14. All contract final accounts are subject to checking and certification by a quantity surveyor.	
		15. All contract final accounts are subject to attestation audit by internal audit who check performance against contract conditions.	

Table 3.5 *(contd)*

Control objectives	Control reference *(see Flow chart)**	Test	Comments and cross reference to working papers
	Point 33	16. a 'performance bond' of 10% is required from the successful contractor;	
	Point 34	17. a retention of 10% is made until the expiry of the 'defects' period;	
		18. provision for liquidated damages is enforced.	
	Page 4 Point 40	19. All site visits by architect/ engineer/quantity surveyor are recorded and signed in site visit log.	
	Point 43	20. All contracts over 3 months duration have monthly progress reports filed by clerk of works.	
		21. All contracts have a post-completion assessment report signed by an architect or engineer not responsible for contract letting or performance prior to payment of final account.	

*not reproduced herein

the matrix illustrated in Table 3.7 immediately highlights any potentially risky areas.

In this case high risks are indicated by two tests in the wages system. The matrix also gives some measure of overall comparison between systems – the average score. By comparing the results of such checklists over several years a relatively comprehensive fraud risk profile of each main system might be constructed.

Table 3.6 Substantive test programme grants for tree planting

Prepared by: . . . . Reviewed by: . . . . Encl. Ref: . . . .
Date: . . . . Date: . . . . File Ref: . . . .
Programme Objective: To gain direct substantive evidence of the accuracy, completeness and validity of the grant payments.

Tests objectives	Control reference*	Test†	Comments and cross-reference to working papers
	File H/3/3	Examine application forms; selected on a judgemental basis to cover the whole year and all areas of Riscashire. Check that	

Only eligible applicants are approved for grant	H. 17	1. Applicant is eligible according to statutory requirements (set out in H17). In particular:	See Working Paper 4C
		(i) trees are of species listed;	
Paper		(ii) location is close to a public highway (check with OS	Working
		map attached);	4E
		(iii) land is not adversely affected by local plans.	
	H.19	2. The applicant owns the land (see copy of title) or is a tenant with fixed leasehold of at least 25 years unexpired.	
	H.23	3. The applicant has certified and dated the claim.	
Grant is in accordance with laid-down condition and calculated correctly	H.25	4. An initial inspection report was prepared and signed by a senior officer to recommend or amend the applicants claim and planting proposals prior to Committee approval.	
	H.26	5. Committee approval (land and amenity) was given and that budget was not exceeded. Check the arithmetic of the grant claim and agree to committee approval for £X for the individual named.	
Grant is given to correct applicant for agreed works	H.28	6. Expenditure listed on output tabulation under code H21573-B agrees for each grant selected – name, amount, address and brief description.	
	H.35	7. A post completion report was prepared and signed by a senior officer other than the one at 4 above no sooner than 12 months after the payment of grant. This report confirms the locations, species and area covered agree as per original grant application and inspection report.	
		8. Inspect a selection of sites and compare to initial inspection report.	

*not reproduced herein
†tests 3, 4 and parts of 5 and 7 also relate to the compliance test programme

Table 3.7

Systems test selected	1st	2nd	3rd	4th	5th	nth	Average
Debtors	0	0	0	1	0	0	0.29
Cash collected	0	0	0	0	0	0	0.13
Creditor	0	0	0	0	2	0	0.31
Central purchasing	0	0	1	0	0	0	0.09
Salaries	0	0	1	0	0	0	0.03
Grants (trees)	0	0	0	–	–	0	0.00
Wages	0	5	4	0	0	0	1.25
Grants (students)	0	0	0	0	0	0	0.03
Loans	1	0	0	0	2	0	0.27
Capital works (roads)	0	1	0	0	0	0	0.73
Investments	0	0	0	–	–	0	0.00

Concluding points

It was necessary at the beginning of this chapter to outline the systems-based approach to audit for the benefit of non-auditors. The adapted version of the systems-based approach enables the auditor or manager to concentrate on those aspects most generally useful in preventing fraud and corruption either during the audit or towards the close of the audit when most of the evidence from testing is available.

The three case studies have been set within typical audit situations which have been chosen to illustrate how weaknesses in the system may lead to examples of fraud and corruption. It is most important that the manager or auditor appreciates not simply how the examples arose in the case studies but what should have been done to prevent any repetition.

The overall message of this chapter is that a well-planned and well-executed systems-based audit encourages a secure system and will go a long way towards preventing fraud and corruption.

4

Capital projects and major contracts

Introduction

This chapter is mostly about major capital works contracts. These contracts account for the vast bulk of normal capital expenditure, whether funded initially from capital or from revenue sources.

Another main group of contracts, on-going revenue contracts, are not considered in this chapter because for our purposes they are more akin to ordinary purchases and creditor payments dealt with in Chapter 6. The main difference is usually no more than replacing the usual order by a more formal and detailed contract, entered into at the start of the contract period. The supply of gas, water, lift maintenance or whatever will usually be invoiced in the usual way and should be checked, and the risks of fraud considered, in the same way as for a one-off delivery of fuel oil or light bulbs.

Contracts for compulsory or voluntary competitive tendering for service provision or for facilities management are becoming an important issue throughout the public sector. Sometimes politicians and indeed the officers are surprised to find that most public sector organizations have had many years' experience of competitive tendering, at least from the client stand-point, long before compulsory competitive tendering (CCT) became fashionable. Additional care will be required to define the precise needs of the body, to draw up the CCT tender specifications and to evaluate the tender proposals. But the basic structure and safeguards developed to deal with capital works contracts, particularly in respect of inviting tenders, have usually been in place for some time in most organizations with any sizable capital budget. These are outlined in Figure 4.1 and can usually be adapted to deal with most CCT situations.

Major capital works contracts

These usually take up by far the most time in contract design, vetting, control and audit work. For many organizations they are of much greater value than any other single area of expenditure, capital or revenue. At the risk of tarring too many with too broad a brush, it is often said that capital works contracts nearly always involve relatively high risks of corruption. The amounts of money (and potential profits) are very high and quite often a lucrative public sector contract can mean the difference between financial success or ruin for a company. In these circumstances the pressure that can be brought to bear upon public servants and their political masters may be enormous.

Any major capital contract from irrigation schemes to road building, but particularly building works, can be split into ten convenient headings. These are discussed as this chapter progresses.

The headings often cover activity over several years, from establishment of needs to past contract assessment. Anyone, manager or auditor, seeking to prevent fraud and corruption should consider all stages. Unfortunately familiarity with all stages of a project is unlikely to be maintained by a single manager. (Figure 4.1 outlines in very broad terms the main activities covered under the headings excluding freedom of information and planning issues which are considered in the text.)

Establishment of needs

This is essentially a political stage although in practice many of the needs are of an uncontroversial and often recurring nature. A good example of these are cyclical building maintenance works which may be almost permanently enshrined as part of a basic property maintenance strategy. Very few politicians would question the need to maintain valuable housing stock, schools, hospitals, office buildings, drainage facilities, etc. whether they ultimately intend to retain or dispose of these assets.

The need for new capital works – hospitals, sea defences, military installations, roads, tunnels or whatever – is, in contrast, often highly controversial.

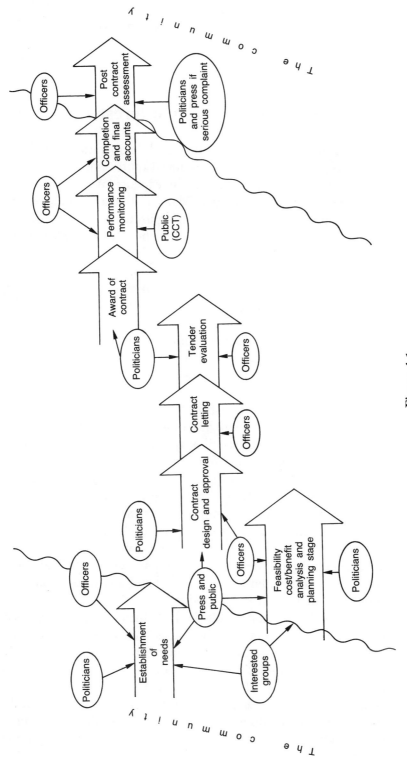

Figure 4.1

Political debate on such new works may well extend to any future capital and on-going revenue implications.

Freedom of information to interested parties

Provided debate is informed, open and democratic the risk of corruption in the conventional sense can be reduced quite significantly. It may be argued that a project will benefit few at the expense of many, or that it is an act of unjustified waste, or whatever. Many politicians interpret the deeply held views of others to be, say, a corrupting influence on society, or harmful to the natural environment. Such stances cannot be ignored, but they are outside the scope of this work and it is left to the reader to exercise his or her own values and principles. Nevertheless, the opening up of debate on the needs, costs and motives of a capital project to close political scrutiny can act as a deterrent to overt favouritism and various other corrupt practices.

Occasionally public officials may encounter significant attempts or pressures to stifle factual information – information that, if it is not covered by the Official Secrets Act, would normally be openly available to the press and public. Such attempts to stifle information may well be driven by financial corruption.

At this point it is interesting to consider the oft-mentioned differences between central government and most other public sector organizations. Any organization is likely to recoil at the thought of its errors, omissions, follies and (assuming they occur) frauds or acts of corruption being made public. Those in positions of power may try to bring pressure to bear to stifle embarrassing information. Central government bodies can bring serious threats of prosecution and imprisonment to bear on any insiders who release such information – consequences that reach over and above any of the more usual threats such as loss of current job or promotion prospects. This undoubtedly places central government departments and the ministers in charge of them in a far more powerful and less accountable position vis-à-vis corruption than other public bodies.

It is true that in other public bodies officials, acting perhaps under pressure from political members or appointees, may also act to suppress information that would otherwise be treated as being in the public domain. But, apart from a very few exceptions (such as sections of the Local Government Act 1972 applying to council meetings where matters relating to the confidential affairs of individuals or companies are to be discussed) the law gives more support for the freedom of information from other public bodies and makes suppression of embarrassing information more difficult than would otherwise be the case. For example the Data Protection Act 1984 guarantees the right of access to computerized personal records in most circumstances under which these are held. The Local Government (Access to Information) Act 1985 also gives the public certain rights of access to local government.

The important question in most circumstances is: does the act of withholding information constitute or encourage fraud and corruption as generally understood and defined by the acts discussed in Chapter 1? The dividing line between corruption in a financial sense for personal monetary gain and corruption in a more general political sense is easy to miss. In the public sector the manager and the auditor must be sensitive to this distinction.

Planning and related issues

This question of withholding information is part of a wider question of taking corrupt or unfair advantage of information, whether or not it is eventually released. Large-scale developments that require planning permission and are subject to building control regulations will involve tenderers in complex exercises estimating the costs of work to arrive at their final bid. The officers handling such developments can have access to valuable information which should be kept secure at all times.

An obvious conflict of interest arises if a politician or public servant has a fiduciary interest in any of the companies attempting to obtain planning permission or to estimate the costs of work or the value of rival bids. Many of the examples of fraud involve collusion between private firms and public servants. Such hidden interests are virtually impossible to uncover, unless things go wrong for the colluders (or their friends, colleagues, family, etc.) and they start talking to the press, police, senior managers or others. Various official lists of the interests of politicians are indeed held. Public servants are generally required to declare any interests they or their immediate family may hold in outside firms who do business with public bodies. But it is very unlikely that anyone, politicians or officials, would declare an interest if they intend to perpetrate a fraud. Of course the requirement for such declarations may have a deterrent value but this value, if it exists, is virtually impossible to measure.

Both freedom of information and, at the planning stage, general publicity and public awareness of interests and intentions, are an inherent, if still limited, safeguard in avoiding the opportunity for corruption. Where appointed members or public officials have it within their own powers to decide on major developments involving large sums of expenditure the risk of corruption is increased. All these considerations apply before the decision to go ahead and they can involve a high level of risk. After this decision the number of opportunities for fraud and corruption are generally increased, though it is often the case that many of these opportunities relate to lower value frauds.

Feasibility and contract design

For new projects these two closely related stages (Figure 4.1) are very important. There are always risks that consultants or in-house professionals will undertake or recommend work that is not really required or recommend specifications that are likely to give advantage to a contractor they favour, possibly their own colleagues. This is particularly so if the client has not set out detailed, clear and unambiguous requirements. To a large extent issues of corruption at this stage of a major project overlap with issues of value for money (VFM). Feasibility should involve a cost benefit analysis – how do differing designs compare? What are the likely future revenue implications of the designs? If good VFM is being achieved the scope for corruption is generally reduced. Specifications that are limited to genuine needs, rather than included merely in the hope of deterring competition with or from particular firms, are more likely to produce a design that is cost-effective. Whether or not the cost can be afforded or is less than the potential benefits (i.e. cost-efficient) is of course entirely another matter, more the concern of the management accountants.

Contract letting

At this stage measures to prevent fraud and corruption change from broad consideration of principle and overall arrangements, such as freedom of information and open debate, to more detailed considerations of individual procedures, in particular procedures that constitute key internal controls.

At the outset of contract letting decisions must be made about the number of firms to be invited and the basis of tender. To some extent the law lays down requirements; for example, European Community directives currently adopted by the UK require contracts over a certain amount to be advertized in the European Journal. The amount is varied over time according to the exchange rate between the pound sterling and the European Currency Unit (the ecu).

Tenders are sometimes invited on a purely open or 'public notice' basis. It is often argued that this is the fairest method. Provided sufficient notice and reasonable details of the value and nature of the work are widely notified in, say, the professional journals applicable to the type of contractors, all contractors who might possibly be interested get a chance to make their interest known. However, unless the work required is of a very specialized nature or the market supply is, for some other reason, hard pressed to meet existing commitments, then most organizations usually restrict detailed tendering to a limited number or 'select list' of contractors. This is often quite reasonable on practical and cost grounds, though the list may well be selected from the most promising replies received from a public notice. For this reason the selection procedure must be fully recorded, e.g. by committee minutes, and seen to be fair. Quite often the replies to any initial notice will be sent a project specification, including computer hardware requirements, building designs and materials, safety requirements and so on, depending on the nature of the work. At this stage some initial respondents may withdraw.

Sometimes permanent select lists are maintained of firms who are approved for work within certain categories and to certain cost limits. All or some firms may be chosen from the lists by various selective methods. At this point it is not difficult to see the risk of corruption starting to increase. How does a firm get approved? How does a firm move from a relatively minor list for, say, small value property repairs to major construction projects? Who selects the firms to be invited to tender from the current list? Who decides the criteria for regular selection? Who decides when a firm is dropped from a list and the reasons? The issue of who makes such decisions – an individual senior officer, a group of officers, a committee – becomes less critical the more the reasons for the decision are fully documented and guided by objective criteria.

Consider for a moment the relative risks of a senior officer, perhaps an architect, accountant or engineer, or perhaps a 'generalist' civil servant who is given complete freedom to choose firms (or even a single firm where market response is slow or unpredictable). Compare these risks to the risks where he or she (or they) are required at least to:

1. include in a list any company given a positive financial vetting by an independent party, e.g. auditors or credit rating agencies;
2. include the company that won the last similar contract let and was not significantly penalized for poor work or failing to meet deadlines;
3. include at least four other firms on a rotating basis so that all the list is covered over a given number of projects, years, etc.

and so on depending upon the nature, value and complexity of the work, past histories and any legal requirements.

In both the private and the public sector practical requirements and past experience often dictate the need to select firms to tender. But in the public sector, often lacking a motive to maximize or optimize profits, the old adage about 'all power corrupting and absolute power corrupting absolutely' is particularly apposite. If this seems to necessitate a less efficient organization bound more than most by red tape the appearance is a short-term view. In the long run dishonesty in public sector affairs usually leads to even greater inefficiencies than a little red tape. The important point is not who selects firms to tender or even if every possible interested firm is invited. Rather it is how the selection is undertaken and how it can be shown to be fair. Impartiality must be shown from the decision to use contractors for all or part of a project to the compilation of a short list, to the final awarding of the contract, whether two or 200 tenders are received. To help achieve this, certain procedures and precautions are (or should be) virtually standard throughout all public bodies.

1. The tender should be in a standard form for all tendering firms. In many building and engineering works standard forms are issued by the Joint Contracts Tribunal (JCT), the Institution of Civil Engineers (ICE) or the government where conditions such as Government Conditions – GC/Works/1/2 etc. – are used. These certainly make it less likely that disputes will arise and the room for fraudulent behaviour (by either party) is reduced. However non-standard tenders are also used especially for projects at the upper end of the cost scale or where the client does not have requirements normally catered for by building and engineering works contracts. Projects of a 'design and build' nature are becoming increasingly popular particularly among local and health authorities. In this case the final specification that would otherwise have been part of the standard tender documents varies between each contractor according to the design. Various gradations of specifications from basic building specifications laid down by an in-house design team to short policy-type statements may be used. An important point in minimizing risks of corruption is that identical initial specifications are given to each contractor at the same time.

2. Any pre-tender site visits should be strictly controlled and open to all contractors. This is also true when tendering for service contracts such as cleaning, leisure services or catering. If all contractors are not shown the whole site and conditions at the same time or at least subject to the same facilities and constraints over inspection some are likely to complain at a later date that they were treated unfairly. This precaution is rather in the same vein as freedom of access to information mentioned earlier.

3. If a contractor requires additional information and this request is granted, the same information should, for obvious reasons of equity, be sent to other contractors.

4. All tenders should be received by a specified deadline and held securely and unopened until a specified opening time. Opening should be in the presence of independent officers, i.e. not officers representing any in-house team or involved up to that point in the tendering process. Usually a senior executive, a political member (such as a committee chairman or junior minister) could be expected to be included in membership of a tender committee for major contracts. Some organizations send identical envelopes inside which the tender should be returned, thus hoping to make it more difficult to spot and presumably delay or destroy a particular tender. In practice this is unlikely to occur once tenders have been received and in any event most tender envelopes will have differing postmarks.

5. The tender documents should be signed by all members of the opening committee to avoid any risk of substitution at a later date.

6. The bottom line results are usually summarized and most importantly sent to each firm that asked to tender (without the names of rival bidders). In this way if a tender has been altered or prevented from arriving on time or at all, the firm concerned will be able to raise the alarm.

Tender evaluation

Contract letting merges into tender evaluations as soon as the details of the bids or the presentations of the schemes are known. Evaluation may be a brief arithmetical exercise to find the contractor with the lowest cost or highest offer. However even fairly simple cases can involve casting and cross-casting rates and bills of quantities to ensure the final summary used to compare each contractor is arithmetically correct. If this is not the case the client organization then needs to decide if any inaccuracies are immaterial and do not affect the result of the comparison. It is not usually considered unfair to contact the contractor for clarification if in the final analysis it is merely his arithmetic or typing that is in question, always provided he is not given any indication of the results of the tender comparison.

At the other extreme, evaluation of tenders can be complex and highly subjective. Cost benefit techniques may help give politicians and other decision-makers an idea of the measurable costs and benefits involved in, say, a design and build scheme. But different contractors may submit different designs and in any event many of the matters finally debated by political members are unlikely to be easily quantifiable. Hence in all but the most simple of schemes evaluation is thrown back into the political arena and freedom of information and open debate should once again provide a measure to help prevent fraud and corruption.

It is often the case that questions of corruption arise some time after any debate or evaluation. For this reason any evaluation, particularly any cost/benefit analysis should be fully recorded as should the minutes of debates. Any accusation however apparently trivial should be documented together with the action taken. These measures are as much for the benefit of the parties accused as any reply to the party making the accusation.

Contract awarding

The actual awarding of a contract might appear a simple matter of writing to successful bidders and notifying them of their good fortune and the date from which the contract is to commence. But even here risks can arise.

If the start date has not been set out precisely in the specifications any delay could prove costly. Even if it has, only a severe delay is likely to be worth a retender. Quite a high proportion of building contracts are delayed at the start. These initial delays and any subsequent delays may be the subject of claims for 'liquidated damages' usually at so much per day. Site access, working conditions and disturbances to nearby land and property should, ideally, all be covered in the contract. It is surprising how, once the contract has been awarded, ironing out arrangements for such items as works sanitations, hours and conditions of work, commencement date, access to site by client employees, etc. can lead to costly delays. It might be asked: what have these issues to do with fraud and corruption? Hopefully, not much. Yet the dividing line between poor drafting or poor management and deliberate and possibly fraudulent delay is often difficult to define.

Performance monitoring

Similar difficulties in interpretation and measurement can arise throughout the monitoring of a contractor's performance. The split between the client and the contractor(s) must be maintained at all levels if a public sector body is not to be accused of unfairness and corruption. Throughout the period of the contract the client officers will come under pressure, often from former colleagues and others with whom they have done business for many years, to overlook contractor error, agree to extensions of time, etc. Disputes will arise between client and contractor as to the nature of the blame for, say, delays or poorly provided services. It is common practice to issue warnings and penalty points against a contractor for failing to meet such performance standards as response times in emergency work, meeting completion dates, and various quality measures. In these circumstances certain key controls should be in place throughout the period of the contract.

Separation of duties between client and contractor

This may seem obvious beyond need of reiteration, but many contractors offer consultancy and other expert-related services in design and management of contracts. If the client is tempted to employ these or is unaware of the links between an apparently independent consultancy and a contractor then serious conflicts of interest will arise. Separation should be maintained when an in-house team such as a works Direct Services Organisation, 'DSO' wins the contract. Separation may be more difficult when client and contractor staff share the same premises but, unless it is decided not to invite other contractors, then a lack of separation will almost invariably give rise to accusations of bias and unfairness if not of outright fraud. This is particularly so when certifications, such as for 'variation orders' are prepared and a quantity surveyor, architect or engineer certifies the reasons for extra work. All such measurements and calculations must be done independently of the contractor.

Site visits

Details of all site visits by client managers, auditors or other non-contractor experts should be fully documented, signed and dated. In any later dispute such records may, though not compiled for the purpose, shed important light on an argument. This is in any event good management but the lack of properly documented inspection is a great encouragement for any potential fraudsters.

Management reports

Regular and timely management reports (including summaries of cost against budget, variation orders, extensions, claims for damages, betterments and quality controls, etc.) should be received and evidenced as to the action taken. The first sign of fraudulent activity is often failure to meet work schedules or overruns of cost without reasonable explanations or even without signed variation orders or time extensions. Even worse, contract management may rely upon exception reporting, usually by professionals who themselves may rely upon exception reporting by their juniors. The great disadvantage of exception reporting is that the reporting official is required to stick out his or her neck and carry the full blame for drawing attention to poor or corrupt practices among their colleagues. This is entirely different and requires a great deal more independence and strength of character than making out a regular report that is a normal part of one's job. The main advantage of exception reporting applies to automated or regular processes whereby (assuming exception does not become the norm) senior managers are usually forced to act.

Exception reporting on major contracts is not like exception reporting on automated industrial or clerical processing. On major contracts time budgeting and production measurement involve considerable subjective judgement and an unplanned overrun can often be genuinely unforeseen and no cause for alarm. The precise stage of completion of a major building work can rarely be specified to the same level of precision as the production of a mechanical component or the processing of a benefit claim. This is even more the case where major public works are of an unusual nature, indeed possibly unique. For these reasons regular management reporting is generally of more value in combating fraud and corruption than exception reporting provided of course management take properly recorded action.

Site records

Site records should be up to date and available for inspection. Site visits – arranged with senior management – should be at short notice and all records should be available for inspection. Inspection details will vary enormously between contracts but some attempt should be made to verify stage payments to date and work in progress.

Deliveries

Deliveries to site, requisition from stores and stock control of site stores should be authorized and controlled as described in Chapter 6. Basically all deliveries, stock measurements and any damages/returns should be subject to signed authorization with appropriate delegations of value.

Performance bond

It is fairly standard practice for the contractor to provide a performance bond. This is unlikely to prevent or deter fraudulent actions but may provide some recompense if a fraud on the part of the contractor can be proved to have had a detrimental effect on the client.

Unusual payments

Various unusual payments and claims, e.g. for unforeseen circumstances, ex gratia amounts, direct payments from client to subcontractors, should be treated with caution and only authorized by the highest level of client management. If monies are being paid that were not even envisaged in the original contract then the chain of public accountability from politician, via the officers acting as client to the contractor may be broken. In short anything that does not come within the direct scope of the 'bill of quantities', 'certified variation orders' under the term of the original contract or any specifications forming part of the original contract should be fully explained and agreed by senior managers and, if significant, by political members.

Completion and final accounts

Final accounts, despite being the accounts of the contractors, may be prepared by senior in-house specialists such as quantity surveyors or third party consultants. This is one significant area where internal auditors may undertake attestation audit, i.e. they attest or certify the accuracy of accounts. (Major claims by or accounts of subsidiary organizations are other less frequently encountered examples.) In most situations quantity surveyors, engineers and architects of the client (or their consultants) and interim audit work will provide documentary evidence to back up the final account sums. Site visits, if appropriate, will have been undertaken during the currency of the contract as will audit of any interim certificates. Ideally, the auditors' involvement will have been intermittent throughout the contract period at key stages to test the controls identified so far. (Auditors sometimes refer to this as current contract audit or CCA for short.)

For major capital projects CCA is very desirable, but unless an audit section is exceptionally well resourced or few capital contracts are undertaken a CCA approach may not be feasible on all capital contracts. Nevertheless, attestation of the final accounts can still provide a worthwhile insight into the likelihood of irregularities in the tender evaluation and performance of the contract. Unfortunately, earlier stages, such as the need for the project, the suitability of the design and the selection of contractors invited to tender, are often beyond any significant independent appraisal at this late stage.

With the likely need in mind to delve as far back as possible prior to the final accounts stage the checklist in Appendix 4.1 was compiled. The final accounts work carried out by the auditor and indeed by the quantity surveyor preparing the account is basically one of checking arithmetic and facts. Are all rates in accordance with original bills of quantities? have all subtotals been brought forward to summary schedules and ultimately to the final account itself? Readers particularly interested in this aspect of the work or of the wider considerations of auditing major contracts are referred to the Further Reading section

It is difficult to pick out particular checks that guard against fraud and corruption at this final accounts stage, as the whole of the preparation and audit of the final account is in a sense a control against fraud and corruption but the following items should be particularly noted.

1. Any alteration to the original published contract conditions, schedule of rates, bill of quantities, etc. should be initialled by both parties.
2. Any alterations to the final accounts, interim accounts, variation orders and other documents submitted in support of payment should, unless they are obvious errors of a typographical nature, be initialled as above and explanation provided in writing.
3. All final accounts and interim documentation should be submitted to the client in the original (not photocopies), typewritten or in ink without using erasing fluid.
4. Missing vouchers, particularly in support of variations and time extensions should be investigated and, if at all possible, duplicates sought from contractors/suppliers. If necessary the client should refuse any payment due.
5. Daywork records especially timesheets should be signed by site agents, the clerk of works or quantity surveyor (QS), appointed by the client.
6. Correspondence files should be fully examined, particularly for matters relating to subcontractors' appointments, any complaints and disputes. In particular, any details of negotiations that took place before and after tendering should be available on a correspondence file. It should be standard practice to keep all letters exchanged, quotes, requoted sums and notes of any arrangements agreed by telephone.
7. Quite often sums tendered in the first instance turn out to be higher than the sums estimated and set aside in capital or revenue budgets. A retender could be costly and cause delays, and unless the sums are far above the budget, it may not be worth redesigning the project or searching for finance from other sources. Contractors should be invited to lower their bids, possibly indicating any easily attainable savings they feel could be made in respect of, say, specified materials, delayed start dates, etc. At this point written evidence should be retained that:
   (a) ensures all contractors who originally tendered are given equal opportunity to renegotiate on a fair basis. For example, if one contractor is allowed to substitute a less expensive quality of material all others should be notified of the change in specification.
   (b) ensures none of the contractors are given any details of other tenders or of the relative positions of the different companies.

Post-contract assessment and release of monies

This stage is usually the least well performed. Release of retention monies is often a formality upon certification by an architect or engineer that the capital works have no significant defects, perhaps after minor improvements and rectification are negotiated with the contractor. Yet, though little can (nor should) be done to prevent final payment to contractors in most circumstances, this is the stage at which management should ask: 'Did we make the right decisions during our earlier stages, identifying the needs, the feasibility, and the best contract design? Did we choose the right contractor?' A good letting system does not guarantee the contract is let to the best or even a suitable contractor. Most importantly, does the final product meet the envisaged need? Essentially, such questions are of a value for money or operational nature. But all too often indications of poor VFM are indications of possible fraud and corruption. This point is tackled in more detail in Chapter 9 when we will consider some of the problems of public sector accounting.

Other contracts

Although, traditionally, the audit and investigation of contracts has been directed at capital works these skills are being used increasingly to investigate and assess other major contracts. Most public sector bodies enter into numerous contracts every month if not every day. A purchase order for the supply of stationery or a subscription to a trade journal implies a contract in law and many order forms have contract conditions stipulated on the reverse. It would be folly and extremely poor value to audit all purchases using the same approach as that for capital contracts. But the approach outlined can nevertheless form a sound basis for protecting other major contracts against the risks of fraud and corruption. It would be impossible to consider all types of other contracts for lift maintenance, office cleaning, consultancy work, supplies of computer hardware, software and so on in this chapter. Many are, as explained above, best considered as ordinary purchases. However, additional comments are called for on certain aspects that are widely applicable to contracts not of a capital works nature.

Consultancy contracts

Contracts with firms of specialist consultants pose particular risks in respect of fair appointment and the confirmation of work done. The appointment of consultants may:

1. form part of a larger project (particularly consultant architects, engineers or quantity surveyors as part of a capital works project);

2. be an on-going arrangement for regular work at certain limited times for which permanent employment is uneconomic;
3. be an *ad hoc* commission usually for specific advice in the form of a report.

The appointment of consultants should follow procedures similar to other contractors. Unfortunately consultants are often required at fairly short notice. Their personal relationship with and understanding of the circumstances and requirements of the organization can be of critical importance. This often puts them into a far more specialized relationship with their clients than, say, the average firm of building contractors. Many organizations continue to re-employ consultants on the basis that they understand that body's particular requirements better than a new firm would. A so-called professional relationship is built up that involves trust, a degree of flexibility of working arrangements (especially during unanticipated problems) and the like. As stressed throughout, the public sector manager must bear in mind that he is acting in the interests of the wider community, and as in so many respects already discussed he must be seen to act fairly. Most public sector bodies that use consultants in the regular way described above generate sufficient work to build up a worthwhile relationship with several firms. Moreover, any reasonable consultant is likely to appreciate the position of a public servant as being quite different from, say, that of a local manufacturer. For these reasons it should be normal practice to complete a list of consultants and offer work on a competitive basis. If nationally laid down standard fees are offered by all for the same work then rotation of commissions on a systematic basis can usually ensure that firms where standards fall are no longer invited, without risking any accusation of favouritism. Problems can occur when work of an unusual nature is required. In these cases it is fairly standard practice to ask an appropriate professional body to recommend accessible members from its lists.

Official terms of engagement should be made public and clearly laid out in contracts or exchanges of letters that can be readily checked against the fees charged.

A formal post-assessment should be recorded for each consultancy report or other work, with reasons clearly stated for criticism or recommendation to use or not to use the firm for future works.

Compulsory competitive tendering (CCT)

This form of tendering is peculiar to the public sector. An organization is forced, by law, to invite tenders for different parts of its activities. The underlying rationale depends very much upon one's values and political standpoint. Will CCT increase efficiency by lowering the cost or increasing the quality of public services? Will the community's taxes (taken by force) find their way into the coffers of one or two companies to the detriment and possible bankruptcy of others? Does CCT force public sector bodies to compete in or at least emulate the more efficient free market? Or is it nothing like the free market at all due to the restrictions placed upon the various tenderers especially the public sector bodies themselves? Will savings in the short term lead to ineffectiveness in the long term and, perhaps, eventual high-cost public sector intervention? Or is this view no more than sour grapes? These and many similar questions are beyond the direct remit of this book but the underlying feelings behind them are not. Underlying all attempts to execute the will of the politicians in respect of CCT is a need for fairness. Fairness is a very subjective concept. But if the public official does not act in a way that is generally perceived to be fair and, as far as he or she can ascertain, in accordance with the law, it is almost certain that the official will be thought to be acting corruptly. For these reasons CCT puts public servants in an even more delicate and difficult situation than usual.

Peer pressure is likely to be exerted from colleagues whose jobs are at stake, as is political pressure from elected representatives who may well have staked their political careers upon either the success or the failure of CCT. In such circumstances a rigid separation of duties between the client and contractor's roles is one of the few controls likely to be effective against fraud and corruption. Sometimes it is difficult to identify the client. Ultimately the taxpayer/elector is the client. The minister or committee appointed to oversee the function subjected to CCT is the political client. But for all practical purposes officials must perform the role of the client. They must decide the method of selecting contractors, evaluate the tenders or designs or even, depending upon the nature of the service, evaluate quite different business proposals.

The reasons for the choice of contractor must be made public. For most cases this will be the lowest cost or highest revenue offered subject to varying measures of service quality. The latter can prove to be a potential minefield both politically and professionally. It is often very difficult to even quantify service output in agreed terms. Social services, education, etc. are the oft-quoted examples and, currently, these are not subject to CCT though their support services often are. But even a service as apparently quantifiable and well-established as refuse collection can cause problems when comparisons of output and quality are made. Numbers of collections, times and routes can involve such qualitative factors as the effects on traffic congestion.

For the reader's purposes the important point is not the desirability of CCT or the measures used to judge its success or failure. Rather that measures, particularly of costs (direct and indirect) and performance, should be clearly defined and agreed by political representatives well in advance of drawing up the tenders. Any changes of mind once tenders have been opened or are to be evaluated should be fully and publicly explained and recorded.

The highly charged atmosphere that may surround CCT in some public bodies means that decisions that are normally routine for an officer must be confirmed at the highest level or even outside the body concerned. This might entail advice from lawyers, the advice of an auditor or at least second opinions sought from colleagues in other public bodies.

Summary

Capital projects follow a basic progression as outlined in Figure 4.1. It is essential to encourage free and open public debate and to have public access to information right from the start. Once the needs have become established, strict controls should be enforced over the conditions of contract letting. The final evaluation of tenders should, like the establishment of needs and the design of the project, be subject to open political decisions.

Whether the project is a building, an on-going public service or simple debt collection, a firm separation of duties between the 'client' and the contractor should be maintained. All variations should be fully explained and documented and costs monitored by the client. The final accounts stage is a crucial control, bringing together supporting documentary evidence of all stages of work, though controls of a physical or procedural nature and non-documentary evidence cannot usually be examined at this stage. The end of the project is not the end of its assessment, nor of the risk of fraud and corruption, and management should take steps to ensure that any defects, shortcomings and the like are rectified.

The most risk-prone aspects of a major project are often considered to be:

1. conception and political approval (including granting of planning and building consents) often more associated with pressures on politicians than officers;
2. tendering procedures;
3. certification of work done/variations;
4. recognition of inadequate performance.

Case studies

Possible case studies are very varied in this area, though widescale fraud and corruption in contract performance are, arguably, far more difficult to prove in a court of law than petty purchasing or benefit frauds. The first case illustrates the early stages of needs assessment, conception and planning; the second that of a final accounts examination.

Case study 4.1 Burnum City Council crematorium

The need for a new crematorium had been debated at intervals in the council chamber for the past two years. Burnum was a relatively small compact city with very little land available for additional cemetery spaces. A privately run crematorium already existed but the need for extra capacity was evident and agreed by all political parties. Outline planning permission had been agreed on a site owned by the council. An outline specification was drawn up bearing in mind the size of the site; landscaping; likely throughput (Burnum had a relatively large elderly population especially in the more run-down inner city estates); technical requirements such as height of chimney, access (by car, bus) requirements; and the opinions of local communities and interests.

Advertisements were placed in the relevant professional journals and in the European Journal. The initial response was very encouraging, indeed it was overwhelming. Almost 100 enquiries were received and the detailed specification had to be photocopied many times.

Surprisingly few potential contractors showed much interest in completing the detailed specifications. There was little doubt that, as with most competitive contracts, contractors often seek a detailed specification to familiarize themselves with the market long before they have firm intentions of competing.

In due course three firms sent in detailed specifications completed and priced. The design details within the specification varied and one of the three was felt to be totally unsuitable. Both members and officers agreed that this scheme offered the highest costs with the lowest quality of building and surrounds. Unfortunately the two remaining schemes, while broadly comparable in costs and benefits were both in excess of the budget provision for the scheme. Timescales can be very difficult to predict and costs can rise, often erratically, during the stages of conception, design, planning (including planning permissions), any public enquiry and the detailed mechanics of contract letting. Such a project may well take one or more years to be approved. At first this may seem rather bureaucratic compared to commercial organizations. Political accountability, including the need to report to and obtain approval from committees that may meet only infrequently throughout the year is a major cause of delay. Also there is an element of political unpredictability. In debate, sometimes involving sides only too ready to score points no tenderer or officer can assume the feeling of the politicians will remain as it was. Opinions previously expressed may turn out to be swayed by speeches during debate. In local government, resolutions of committees may still need to be adopted by meetings of the full council during which further debate and delay may occur.

Let us assume, as is often the case, that senior officers are asked to negotiate on behalf of the council with the two applicants with a view to reducing the cost of the scheme to within the budget approvals.

Had several firms all put in tenders for roughly comparable amounts in excess of the budget it would have been more efficient (and probably politically acceptable) to amend the materials, design, timing or other ingredients of the scheme and, despite the increased costs of delay, invite retenders. But with only one or two firms interested negotiation on an individual basis is more cost-effective and not unusual. In local and health authorities this method will generally require suspension of some standing orders and financial regulations to allow senior officers to under-take the negotiations. Such officers will have to tread carefully. In one sense by placing them in the spotlight, so to speak, where their actions are deliberately beyond the norm and invite query, the risk that they will succumb to any corrupt influences (whether from tenderers or of their own volition) is reduced. However, negotiations inevitably give more power and discretion than straightforward arithmetic evaluations and used on a regular basis they introduce significant additional risks. It is from this point onwards that events at Burnum wove a web of corruption.

Three senior officers, an architect, a civil engineer and a quantity surveyor were chosen to conduct the negotiations on the council's behalf.

Company A, a medium-sized company with similar establishments at nine locations throughout the country could only meet the cost restriction with significant reductions in the capacity and landscaping of the scheme. Company B, a smaller, more recently formed company were able to offer a design that met almost all the original requirements but extended the completion time from approximately 12 to 15 months. The officers had no hesitation in recommending company B, which was duly awarded the contract. A year and a half later the half-completed project lay abandoned; Company B was in the hands of the official receiver. The taxpayers of the city were paying about double the original costs of the scheme (partly due to large increases in interest charges) for its completion at short notice by a completely different contractor. Not surprisingly the external auditor's attention became focused on the debacle.

The auditor was, at first, concerned mainly with the VFM implications of the cost overrun. However, as he called for the correspondence files and background information on the contract, and as he started to interview the officers concerned, the following points emerged.

1. None of the contractors were subject to the usual level of financial appraisal. (Bank references were sought but these are notoriously easy to come by.)
2. Company B was basically a 'shell' company set up to take advantage of new business opportunities. No parent company guarantee had been sought. In fact because no financial appraisals had been undertaken officers were able to claim that they had no knowledge of the true nature of company B, which appeared, on the surface, to be a normal trading company. Financial appraisals were not enshrined in the standing orders or financial regulations of the council though most organizations would be expected to undertake at least a company search, seek a credit rating and ask their in-house accountants to review the company's latest annual report and accounts.
3. The figures quoted by company B were exceptionally favourable and the cost was far below that offered by other contractors. A profit share clause was offered to the council for the first five years' trading on condition that the council did not give planning permission for any further new crematoria during that time, a condition that was virtually certain to arise in any event. This clause, though virtually worthless, had probably sounded quite attractive to members and at the time the minutes of meetings revealed that the three negotiating officers had presented it as the 'icing on the cake' of their negotiations.

At first the auditor was tempted to assume nothing worse than incompetence on the part of officers of the council and of the company which had by this time gone into liquidation. However an examination of the capital payments of the scheme revealed that for the first 12 months stage payments had been made on a quarterly basis for work done and certified by the same architect, senior engineer or quantity surveyor (QS) as had been involved in the negotiations. After this time most work had come to a halt. This meant that it was doubtful whether company B's parent had actually lost any significant sum on the bankruptcy of its subsidiary as virtually all the costs to date had been covered. In fact a site visit left the auditor with the general impression that the payments, certified by the QS and engineer, had probably erred well on the side of generosity.

A standard performance bond had been deposited with the bank but the monies were small in relation to the outstanding liabilities to subcontractors and the work still remaining. In any event obtaining possession of the bond would probably require complex litigation.

The auditor was suspicious of company B's role and the motive of the parent company. Suspicions of the role of the negotiating officers also arose. The lack of financial appraisal was difficult to explain. The likelihood was that company B's inexperience in this (or any) type of work would almost certainly have come to light during negotiations.

It was also difficult at first to understand the motive of company B's parent. Eventually this became clear from perusing that company's annual report and in conversation with officers of authorities who had offered, or were proposing to offer, similar contracts for which company B's parent had been invited to tender. This market was particularly difficult to break into without a track record. Few authorities were prepared to offer work without being able to know that contracts had already been won by the company. In fact the site at Burnum had been held up as a model design. The showpiece aspect of the Burnum scheme had, according to company B, been one of the factors in deciding to reduce the cost of its initial tender. This fact in itself is not unusual, but the lack of any concern for the likelihood that the scheme would fail financially most certainly was. As soon as company B had (largely on the basis of the Burnum contract) won a contract for a similarly designed crematorium with another authority at more realistic prices it lost interest in the Burnum scheme. By the time they had won their third contract they were fully prepared to let the Burnum scheme lapse and let company B (effectively set up and assigned merely to that scheme) go into liquidation. The more profitable schemes had already been purchased by the parent company or they had been entered into by that company even though company B had been involved in negotiation and fronted the deals.

In this case it would be very difficult despite the great likelihood of corruption that any of the officers could be successfully prosecuted. However the external auditor may have had the power to surcharge members and officers whom he or she considered to have acted irresponsibly. In this case the officers did not seek parent company guarantees and they signed certificates for work that had been completed in the knowledge that even if the work referred to in the certificates was completed it was virtually worthless. There could have been little doubt that company B could not have fulfilled its contract right from the start. Without the contractual obligation of the parent, or some other party, to support it until more lucrative contracts were won company B was virtually bound to fail.

It is very likely, given the urban environment of Burnum, with relatively high land prices and the higher than anticipated bids from genuine companies that the crematorium project was uneconomic from the start. Burnum City Council should have arranged for the joint funding of a crematorium in another more rural authority, or undertaken the project itself, at a loss, if the local electors were so determined. The members, it seems, wanted to be able to control the development for reasons of civic pride, political ego or whatever. When, despite all odds, company B offered, or appeared to offer, options at a price they could afford they were, like all recipients of hoped-for news, only too willing to believe it.

In this case the main controls absent from the tendering procedure were:

1. financial vetting of companies;
2. parent company guarantees;
3. a more competitive and open form of tendering instead of negotiation by officers.

Other controls, particularly over examination or certification work completed or in progress are also likely to have been inadequate. But any one of the three key procedures mentioned above would have been almost certain to have avoided any serious corruption with the taxpayer having to bail out the partly completed project at vastly inflated costs.

Case study 4.2   Ministry for legal aid

The ministry had decided to computerize its main information recording system. A system requirement specification was drawn up and six major manufacturers were invited to tender. The data was quite straightforward but the access requirements of users were quite complicated. Each user needed to be given access permission to the data at different levels. (A user may not be able to call up on screen any records other than those that he or she needs for their work.) This meant in practice that virtually all officers involved in information processing and reporting would need a separate terminal. Despite this the total cost was not considered excessive.

The company eventually successful in supplying the hardware and software were engaged to provide training. Inevitably, a strong working relationship grew up between this company and the civil servants during the course of the implementation of computerization, based on the trust of the latter and the superior knowledge of the former.

It is often the case that officials, however well they may understand their own needs, are far less well versed in the latest information technology.

The ministry was no exception. In such situations the hardware and software suppliers are in a very powerful position; in this case it was one that they abused.

In fact, despite the initial opinions of the auditors, no serious fraud had, legally speaking, been committed. Nevertheless what took place would undoubtedly have been considered dishonest and devious to say the least.

Quite simply much of the equipment was not what had been ordered. The precise make and model of terminals, disc packs, personal computers and laptops were not made completely clear to any of the staff either during installation or during the training seminars. Everything supplied was, in fact, adequate for the work required and the level of security expected. The system specification was met. The project did not run over budget. No complaints beyond the usual teething troubles were expressed by the ministry. Yet between a quarter and a third of the cost was swallowed up by hardware and software of an inferior quality to that actually agreed in the contract. Slightly earlier versions of software (particularly software for generating interrogation reports designed for *ad hoc* use by management) were provided in place of the latest versions. In some cases managers had subsequently been persuaded to authorize purchase of updated versions by sales staff of the very same company that should have provided this in the first place.

The same principle applied to some of the hardware. The hardware, rather than the software, first brought this fraud to light when a clerical assistant was charged with completing an inventory. The inventory was inspired by a change in accounting principles and the subsequent need to revalue all fixed assets. Normally the supplier company could have expected equipment including IT purchases to be checked only upon delivery. Provided the delivery passed unquestioned and maintenance or replacement of faulty items was promptly carried out, it was very unlikely that the delivery would be queried at a later date.

The clerical assistant compiled the inventory from hardware she found being used at the six ministry sites. Her curiosity was aroused by the fact that not all sites had exactly the same equipment for the same job. She had, in any event, intended to scan quickly through the orders just to make sure no significant single items or numbers of smaller items had been omitted. This she thought might happen if she had not known of a section or been told of any recent deliveries. When she obtained the orders she found to her surprise that neither the orders nor indeed the delivery notes bore out the significant variations in model of equipment between sites and sometimes between offices on the same site.

The company apologized and eventually agreed to replace some of the items called into question. However, it pointed to a minor sub-clause inserted in the contract, though precisely when no one seemed to recall, that allowed it to replace items not immediately available with others of similar quality at the same cost. The clause also provided for the ministry to be notified. This notification, it was claimed, had been sent but a revised and updated version was now being prepared.

Although deliveries were signed for at the ministry by the officers who unloaded and stored the equipment, they were generally unable to verify the order at that point. In fact most hardware was not unpacked until installation and this was often done by the company. Some of the ministry staff had, it later transpired, been aware that they were not getting the very latest versions of the hardware and software supplied. Some even queried this with the company but, most importantly, none of these officers was sufficiently senior to have responsibility for the contract or for any of the IT budget.

It is doubtful if any single officer would have been aware of the fact that the ministry was being fleeced had it not been for the inventory clerk. In fact, given the rapid change in IT technology the same dishonest procedures could have been followed during upgrades. One key (and rather old-fashioned) control was missing from the ministry – adequate checking of delivery to contract or order. This is a commonplace weakness for IT equipment delivered through usual channels. Where complicated and valuable items are involved it is essential they are checked by an in-house expert prior to payment.

Concluding points

This chapter has dealt with the more common contracts and typical capital works projects. The issues implicit in these major areas of expenditure apply throughout an organization, though for smaller projects they rarely come to the fore unless something goes wrong or a major change occurs. Is there a real need for…? If so, how should it be provided and by whom? Can the quality, completeness, and effectiveness be monitored? How, and by whom? Can the cost be monitored against the budget and against alternative sources of provision? These are essentially no more than questions of good financial management but, as Chapter 9 outlines, good financial management is one of the strongest defences against fraud and corruption.

Great stress has, rightly, been laid upon those procedures that are likely to form key internal controls and on those that open up the organization decision-making to public scrutiny and accountability. These are important considerations throughout this book. But of equal importance in guarding against fraud and corruption is substantive evidence of the value, legality, completeness and accuracy of expenditure, income, assets and liabilities. This is particularly true of capital projects and CCT contracts. Officials are always at risk to temptation and pressures. A company that would never consider putting undue pressure on a public official for a few hundred or thousand pounds of revenue expenditure may act differently when many millions of pounds are at stake. Likewise an official that would never consider acting improperly when he can affect the outcome of a mere £1000 purchase may have a change of heart when far larger sums are involved. The sheer magnitude of what is at stake makes it imperative that client management participate directly in monitoring performance and in verification of work done and service quality.

Appendix 4.1   Capital works contracts checklist

Tender conditions

1. Is Tender:
    (a) in standard form? (e.g. ICE, JCT.) If not describe basis of tender and attach copy.
    (b) priced?
    (c) unpriced?
    (d) lowest submitted? (Copy file papers to Audit file.)
    (e) correct or has an error been detected in the tender submission? If yes, has it been dealt with in accordance with the Code of Practice for Single Stage Selective Tendering or any internal regulations?
    (f) signed by contractor and dated?
2. Is a filed record of tender bids signed by an Opening Committee?
3. Have letters been sent to all contractors who were unsuccessful/failed to tender, detailing the amounts bid? Note: letters need not usually be sent to tenderers who have written notifying of their inability to tender.
4. Are there any late amendments to the conditions of contract? If yes, give details and note any amendments to be signed by both parties.
5. Are there specific provisions for:
    (a) Health and safety at work;
    (b) overtime working;
    (c) audit of final accounts and supporting documents/books/accounts of contractor;
    (d) site access and conditions;
    (e) contractor's area, noise, hours of work, etc.;
    (f) works sanitation and accommodation;
    (g) supply of water, electricity and telephones;
    (h) precautions against damage to roads, trees, utilities supply, etc.;
    (i) gifts and unfair inducements;
    (j) monthly accounts;
    (k) new rates (star rates);
    (l) daywork;
    (m) records (site and other);
    (n) sequence, schedules, programme of works;
    (o) repair and construction details;
    (p) materials details;
    (q) accurate identification of sites, buildings, land, plots, etc.;
    (r) checking details against property register if appropriate, e.g. housing maintenance;
    (s) other main provisions – give details.

Review and, if appropriate, comment on each.

Bill of quantities (or schedule of rates, etc.)

1. Preamble/Preliminaries should cover:
   (a) cost of site services;
   (b) cost of temporary works;
   (c) cost of testing of materials or ground/site investigation;
   (d) any other costs that are not proportional to works done;
   (e) charging methods;
   (f) method related charges.
2. Review bill of quantities: compare to standard conditions: note any omissions or additions. Consider general reasonableness of quantities and rates.

Final account/final audit

1. Obtain copies of any interim (current) audit work and include with this file.
2. Record date of receipt of final account and any subsequent related information. Record date of commencement of final audit.
3. Check that a certification of practical/substantial completion has been issued and signed by the quantity surveyor (QS), architect or engineer.

4. *Arithmetical checks (see also Appendix 4.2).*
   Check off final account details and arithmetical calculations against amounts, rates, etc. in bill of quantities. Note:

   (a) errors;
   (b) large variations from the bill;
   (c) whether star rates (if any) have been agreed.

   The following (5–19) should be covered as appropriate.

5. *Prime costs*
   Check that any prime costs of works, materials, etc. agree to values and any percentage of costs agreed in the bill of quantities (the bill).

6. *Provisional sums*
   Check that any provisional sums have been accurately transferred to the final account from the bill of quantities. Check that any adjustments (omissions or additions) are fully supported.

7. *Variation orders* (refer to interim audit working papers where applicable)
Check that any variations are supported by orders signed and dated by architect/engineer/QS. Variations should apply to the requirements of the contract rather than to simple increases/decreases in the measurements laid down in the bill of quantities. Significant increases/decreases should be fully documented. Variations should be costed if significant.

Note: variation may be subject to different methods of measurement from the main contract bill of quantities. Any variation relating to prime costs should be fully supported by subcontractors' invoices.

8. *Dayworks* (refer to interim audit working papers where applicable)
Dayworks should be agreed to a national schedule, e.g. as agreed by a professional institute or to a rate set down in the bill of quantities; For example, the Federation of Civil Engineering Contractors' Schedules of Daywork carried out incidental to contract work (issued 23.8.88).

Check all daywork sheets are certified.

9. *Approved contingencies*
To be treated in the same manner as a provisional sum. These should have been catered for by a fixed sum or an agreed percentage of the tender sum. Check any such percentage if figures are available. Bring to the attention of audit management any contingency items not included at tender stage.

10. *Liquidated damages* (refer to interim audit working papers where applicable)
Commencement date .... Period .... Anticipated completion ......
+ .... extensions.

Agree to rate × week or part week. Rate should be set down in bill of quantities.

Note: liquidated damages are a compensation rather than a penalty.

11. *Retention*
Check calculation of retention (usually a percentage of the value of the work) as specified in the contract, e.g. JCT 5% to practical completion; 2.5% to final completion; ICE 5% for contracts up to £50 000 to a maximum retention of £1500; 3% for contracts more than £50 000; 1.5% after a certificate of completion has been issued and up to the issue of a maintenance certificate.

Check that no retention monies have been released without the QS, architect or engineer having signed a certificate of completion, or a maintenance certificate.

12. *Tax*
    This should normally be excluded from contract prices but check that any tax charges for VAT, fuel tax, etc.:

    (a) are correctly calculated and applied;
    (b) relate only to certified works.

    On completion of the works, adjustments may be made for changing tax rates. These should be agreed to legislation.

13. *Price fluctuations* (normally only large contracts over more than one year)
    Check that the contract is not a fixed price contract. Otherwise a price fluctuation to allow for inflation can be expected. If a price index formula has been agreed recalculate the agreed addition or subtraction checking that the correct values have been used.

14. *Interim certificate* (refer to any interim audit working papers where applicable)
    Check that all interim payments are fully supported by certificates signed by the QS, architect or engineer. Check that items included in the certificate are also included in the bill of quantities and/or agreed variations. (See also item 7 above.)

15. *Claims for unforeseen circumstances*
    These should be agreed by the architect/engineer/QS and after checking any supporting documents and calculation they should be brought to the attention of the audit management.

16. *Ex gratia claims* (including claims for compensation)
    These should be brought to the attention of the audit management.

17. *Direct payments to un-nominated subcontractors or other third parties*
    These should be brought to the attention of the audit management.

18. *Payments to nominated subcontractors*
    These should be checked to the original tender/bill of quantities as for normal payments.

19. *Payments for betterment*
    These are received from third parties for betterment of their existing assets or other conditions, e.g. rail bridges.

20. Date final account audited ....

    Balance due .... to contractor.

    Balance owed .... by contractor.

21. Final certificate or expiration of period of maintenance for completion and release of retention monies checked arithmetically and agreed to terms in contract.

Appendix 4.2 Final contractor's account audit – arithmetical checks

Enclosure Ref: ....

File Ref: ....

1. Trace all item descriptions and rates from the original bills of quantities to the final account.
2. Check build-up of all item rates where shown.
3. Check all extensions (quantities × rates) including any supporting sheets.
4. Cast extensions to compare with page totals (ensuring that credits where appropriate are deducted).
5. Ensure correct page totals are carried to the section bill summaries.
6. Trace correct section bill summaries to final account summary and cast.
7. Ensure that the correct total figure is the one certified by the engineer/architect.
8. Agree total payments to date to capital ledger/record of capital payments.
9. Check interim payments listed on ledger to interim certificates issued. Certificates should be signed by the engineer, QS or architect.
10. Any separate invoice for consultants' fees should be agreed to the rate (usually a percentage of the contract value) and the type of work specified in an exchange of letters or contract. (An additional audit programme may be used for consultants.)

5

Information technology

Introduction

This chapter considers various effects of information technology upon the measures needed to guard against fraud and corruption. It also considers the legislative framework that has come about over the past decade in an attempt to bring the law in line with technology though this framework stretches beyond the narrower criminal concerns of fraud and corruption. As with Chapter One an appendix is used to set out key aspects of the legislation.

The subject would without doubt merit a separate work of its own. Computer related fraud can be intermingled with any of the circumstances considered in other chapters as some of the case studies show. This chapter seeks to draw attention to specific fraud prevention measures related to computers and to consider some, often fairly traditional, measures in a computerized working environment.

Why should computers demand special attention?

After all, most significant systems are computerized especially in the public sector. The general systems-based audit approach, identifying key controls that help lessen the chances of a fraud occurring or remaining undetected, can be applied equally to both manual and computerized systems, or to a mixture of both.

Computers can sometimes hide actions more effectively than written records. They can be more easily defended both against unauthorized access and, more worryingly, against management control and accountability. Frequent changes in technology are difficult to keep up with, offering added scope for the criminal mind. Such changes may place the corrupt official in a more exploiting and less accountable position.

Many frauds, especially those involving the unauthorized transfer of funds by computer, can be perpetrated far more speedily than would be the case prior to computerization.

Computer-related fraud tends to be perpetrated by trusted employees, often disgruntled, whose superiors or peers have not previously envisaged information technology being used in such a way. Computer technology is still relatively new as well as being in a constant state of change. Each advance in technology may present additional risks or enable extra safeguards. The objectives and motivations of the fraudster remain the same, or almost so. Some evidence points to the human ego and a misplaced sense of challenge as additional motivations in computer crime, a point we will discuss later.

Every three years since 1981 the Audit Commission for Local Authorities and the National Health Service in England and Wales has published a wide-ranging survey of computer fraud and abuse (see Further reading). The latest survey in 1990, shows a trend for computer fraud to be greatest amongst the purchases/creditors functions which follows the trend for fraud generally. Input-related frauds are by far the most serious. A newly recognized form of computer abuse, the computer virus, accounts for a third of total incidents reported in the survey.

The vast majority of computer-related fraud and abuse, as defined by the Commission, relates to white collar, usually inside, staff. About a third of all incidents were perpetrated by managerial and supervisory officers which highlights the need for detailed review and managerial effort in relation to recruitment, control and counselling of staff.

The remainder of this chapter cannot provide a proven methodology for preventing particular crimes in particular installations. But by directing attention to special features and giving extra prominence to well-tried preventative controls, it seeks to limit the occurrence of premeditated computer-related fraud.

Segregation of duties

This type of control recurs in any computerized system involving financial transactions or the movement of assets. The following is usually an essential separation of duties among the work undertaken on a medium to large installation.

User	Data entry/user at terminal or linked personal computer.
Programmer	Protection and maintenance of operating systems, software and hardware; development and amendment of programmes.
Operator	Handling and custody of value documents such as cheques or licences.
Operator	Data updating and security, including any library, holding, or distribution function.

Segregation is a genuine problem for many relatively small sites or so-called open systems involving computer networks of linked PCs or terminals connected to a secondary processing unit. Supervision, strict password control and a readable, non-erasable audit trail may overcome the risks inherent in a lack of separation in most cases. However, lack of separation can increase the risks of collusion and this is one of the most difficult methods of fraud to detect.

Following transactions around the computer

This involves checking actual payments, transfer of assets, etc. processed by the computer against the prime documentation evidencing the reasons and authority for the transaction. Be above board and open about this – it may well have a deterrent effect.

The computer output, in particular hard-copy reports, can often be verified in total, or with minimal problems of reconciliation, to another computer-produced or manual output of a feeder system that provides the input to the computer. For example, with a payroll system, see Figure 5.1.

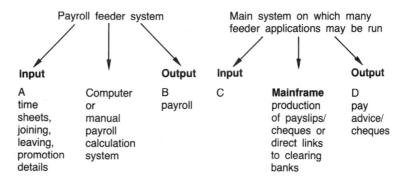

Figure 5.1

A mainframe computer, as shown in Figure 5.1 would usually be used for a variety of other purposes each with its own feeder system. An ideal verification may take place between A and D either in total or on an individual sample basis. Most systems are capable of some reconciliation between B and C or D, as in most systems the relevant management, e.g. the payroll supervisor, or the accountant at the next level above, would need to know that his or her instructions to, say, pay 5000 staff a total of £4 732 000 were followed once they had left the feeder system. Verification, whether in total or on a sampling basis, should be conducted confidentially but openly and above board. Staff, including any potential fraudsters, should know that regular and unpredictable checks are carried out but that all their personal information is treated in the strictest confidence.

The same overall reconciliations between systems should be undertaken for other main transactions, such as debtors, creditors, etc. This element of control is discussed again in Chapter 9 on the main accounting arrangements.

Data input arrangements

However many computerized systems are used to process data, at some point an original input of manually provided information or raw data will have initiated the processing. It may be that this initial input data will be supplied from computer-produced documents provided by, say, an outside supplier. But at initial input no direct link between computer systems will exist. This initial input stage is one of the most vulnerable to fraudulent manipulation. These risks require preventative controls that cover at least the authorization and initial vetting of raw data.

The authorization of input

This should be done by the user at a defined level of responsibility and in a form that cannot be amended or overwritten. Signed hard-copy vouchers, printout produced from a feeder system or input control sheets are often the most secure. Ideally, input totals produced from manual or computerized feeder systems should be capable of being easily and directly cross-checked to output totals produced by the system that has been updated, i.e. cross-checked from A to B and B to D in Figure 5.1.

Initial vetting

Data should be subject to immediate validation checks as soon as they are input. These may, for example, include checks over maximum or minimum monetary values for individual transactions; agreement of the total values or numbers of items against a batch total for organizations where batch processing is still in operation; comparison of input records to lists of unacceptable parameters such as blacklisted addresses or unacceptable transaction dates. Whatever the procedures for programmed vetting of data, generally speaking the sooner this is undertaken the less risk of fraud.

Data updating and processing

The data that are input will usually be used to update standing information on suppliers, debtors, rent accounts, etc. It is crucial that access to this standing data, or master files as they are often called, is securely controlled. If standing property details, rent accounts, tax accounts, etc. are deleted or interfered with the fraud may run into millions of pounds and go completely unnoticed for an indefinite period. By comparison, for the transaction data being input, an unauthorized interference would usually have to be repeated and risk detection time and time again to create comparable mayhem.

Ideally, the data user should monitor or carry out regular checking of the information held on the standing data master file. This may be difficult especially where the user is a small department with little time available for review or checking, or a user-friendly print of the master files data may be difficult to obtain. In any event the master file and the arrangements and controls covering amendments thereto should be regularly reviewed by a senior programmer, analyst or computer auditor not involved in the design of the operating system or the application to which the master file relates.

During an updating run of a major mainframe processing system, say a weekly or monthly payroll run, programming and system design staff should be kept clear of the operation. This involves a standard separation of duties between operating staff (including data preparation, input and control officers) and programming staff. This separation of duties often breaks down on a day-to-day basis as programmers are consulted about malfunctions in software they helped design or install. In practical terms, given the tendency of many organizations to move away from batch processing mainframe situations to networks and PC-based systems, this control is often difficult to impose. Nevertheless every time the separation breaks down the potential risk of fraud is increased, as indicated by the increasing computer crime statistics. Management should consider what other controls can compensate for the lack of separation of duties.

Among the other possible controls are regular reviewing of management control information related to:

1. programme amendments;
2. data amendments;
3. access (or unsuccessful access attempts) to live data especially during updating runs.

Additional supervision and the encryption coding of sensitive or valuable data to be transmitted or updated are other possible control features that may compensate for inadequate separation.

Data access and output

Final output (as opposed to intermediate output to magnetic media used for further updating) can be on screen, on printed hard copy, or even be recorded voice output.

Screen output is largely controlled via access controls that apply to input and output at a terminal or PC screen. Access control is very much dependent upon physical security of the terminal PC and password protection over the software.

Quite often a read-only facility is available to numerous users and has a relatively low level of password protection. The risk is often that relatively junior officers who would be denied access to sensitive manual records or hard-copy reports, will have access to data from which the reports were compiled. Even if no fraud is possible, the Data Protection Act (1984) must still be borne in mind and personal data should not be released to users who do not have a genuine and legal right of access, see page 129.

Exception reports

In Chapter 4 we mentioned some of the drawbacks from which exception reports suffer in respect of capital works programmes. Capital projects are varied; each one is usually quite different from others even when they are of a repeatable nature such as housing improvements. Computerized bulk processing of transactions and on-line updating of standing information are, however, events of an on-going type with little variation in nature. In fact, many of the uses of a computerized system are akin to the industrial production-line processes and lend themselves to the use of exception reports as a mean of internal control; for example, computer production of payroll – summary reports, payslips, cheques, etc. – or of stock item movements – purchases, issues, returns and stock-in-hand – or of hospital bookings; in fact most types of regularly required information. For these types of information exception reports can play a useful role as a key control. The regular monitoring of progress, as used in respect of major capital developments, may become a useless mass of statistics. In such circumstances management would normally wish to view only the exceptions and the overall trends. In these circumstances exception reporting may well be the only practical answer. Indeed effective management is often characterized by the ability to discern the important exception reports and interpret what they mean. Thus, taking the examples mentioned above, exception reports of payroll payments over a certain value, high volume stock movements or trends in emergency bed usage may be a useful internal control. Exception reports may well accompany key trend totals such as monthly management accounts or, say, bed or stock usage totals.

Action and relevance

For exception reports and any other computer output to be an effective form of control they must be relevant and actioned. This may seem too obvious to be worth saying yet in many IT frauds information that may have prevented or at least ended a fraudulent activity was delayed until it was no longer relevant, directed to an irrelevant destination, produced in an irrelevant or unintelligible form or simply available but not actioned. Lapses in checking computer usage logs are examples of failures to action output.

Security of output

The security of output (in whatever form) should be considered in the wider context of its relevance and who should action it. Since the Data Protection Act 1984 additional weight has been given to the relevance and security of the output of personal data. Confidential hard-copy output should be re-corded and, if necessary, signed for by the intended recipient.

Various security measures include:

1. password control for access to screen output;
2. printers located in a high-security area;
3. logging of all copies of reports and their intermediate and final destinations;
4. separation of duties between output production/distribution and any officers employed earlier in the data input and processing stages. In practice such a separation may be either among the most difficult to achieve or achieved automatically when output is on-line to users or outside parties. Any relatively small quantity of output that has to be physically distributed is unlikely to justify the employment of officers other than computer staff who already have input or processing duties.

Systems development, operation and maintenance

The traditional input-processing-output scenario assumed above is generally discussed as if it operated within a steady state of affairs. This is seldom if ever the case. New systems are being developed and existing systems are being enhanced and maintained all the time. From an auditor's objective it is often permissible to take 'snapshots' of the current state of the system at various audit visits. These may be adequate to help form an opinion of the balance sheet values or the overall reliability of the system's internal controls, particularly if sufficient audit testing is undertaken. But this conventional audit approach offers only minimal assistance in preventing fraud and corruption. If one is determined to prevent or at least keep to an absolute minimum any risk of fraud and corruption then all new developments, user support measures, system enhancements and routine maintenance must be both independently audited and monitored by management. This would require far more effort and resources than a periodic (say annual) audit which is usually directed only at specific applications being run on the system, and more than the usual management checks and controls. Indeed, it is arguable that much more effort would be required to reduce the risk of fraud to a minimal level on a computerized system than on an equivalent manual system, though nowadays this argument is becoming increasingly difficult to prove as so few sizeable systems are not computerized. In a manual system all concerned usually recognize the prime importance of staff attitudes, morale and, quite simply, the way the system is used as a factor in preventing fraud and corruption. In a computerized system far more reliance tends to be placed upon the design of the system (security over access to hardware, or software facilities guarded by complex levels of password control are typical and essential design features). But most computer frauds seem to be made possible by designed controls being allowed to lapse, deliberately by-passed or simply not built into the final system. When a computer, especially a mainframe, is relied upon by those seeking routine reports, calculations, updates on events or whatever, they are largely unaware of the attitude of its controllers, designers and maintainers. If the same information was being sought from an army of clerks, or even a few key personnel, their attitudes collectively and individually would usually be recognized as crucial. In such non-computerized systems, human attitudes conducive to fraud and corruption are far less likely to remain unnoticed by those seeking information.

All this points towards a need for greater resources if a computerized system is to be secure. But why spend the money? Basically, because computers introduce risks on a magnified scale. Quite often a single relatively junior official may commit crimes or wreak havoc that it would be difficult to have imagined in a precomputerized era. Entire payrolls or other regular payment runs can be duplicated, access to very large sums of money can be gained and used for fraudulent manipulation often via a single password, credit transactions or information highlighting debtors can be surpressed, sensitive information can be 'hacked' and sold. Many examples have come to light in recent years, often involving relatively few fraudsters in each case.

Because risks of computer-related fraud depend very much on attitudes and motivations and these are often obscured by technology, issues concerning the selection and motivation of staff must be given extra emphasis. During any system design or enhancement and when reviewing the controls over system maintenance, including so called 'change control' procedures, senior management should ensure that the new system or changes can at least satisfy the security requirements of the old system, and key personnel involved in design, testing, operating and maintaining the system should be subject to adequate pre-assignment vetting, separation of duties, and performance review (see Assessment of key personnel.).

Computer-related reviews

This short section is intended to act rather like the fraud checklists considered in Chapter 3. Often management are unaware of the risks involved in the computerized system or parts of systems for which they are responsible. It is very important that the management should sometimes be able to stand back from the routine (of ensuring the system output or product is completed and arrives at its intended destination on time) and undertake a fraud risk review along the following three main themes.

1. Review potential financial loss (or embarrassment).
2. Review internal controls in areas highlighted by 1.
3. Review the key personnel (numbers, grade, performance, etc.) in the light of 1 and 2.

Given the specific objectives of combating fraud and corruption each review will probably appear narrower than a full audit or managerial review and will be weighted towards selected key control procedures. Each of the above three themes is considered below.

Loss and sensitivity assessment

An external auditor attempts to assess the 'materiality' of the balance being audited. Thus, for a set of accounts with a balance sheet total of, say, £120 000 000 and revenue expenditure of £90 000 000 over the year, a year-end provision for bad debts of the order of £10 000 would, other things being equal, be immaterial. Of course some audit effort would be required to verify the £10 000 was not hopelessly undervalued but it is unlikely that extensive audit testing or system evaluations would be undertaken on any balance or annual system throughput of less than say 0.005% of £90 m for revenue and £120 m for balance sheet, i.e. £450 000 and £600 000 respectively. The auditor would probably take additional notice of any major system that gave rise to an unexpectedly low value and the potential sensitivity of any particular figures. For example, expenditure directed at subsidizing, say, a controversial local hospital unit may amount to only £250 000 but require special attention by the auditor because a serious over- or understatement could undermine the credibility of the local politicians and call into question the auditors' own attention to sensitive detail.

This brief account of materiality in an external audit context belies the complex professional judgements that may be required to take account of monetary values and perceived risks. Nevertheless it can provide a useful model when applied to computer systems. Every installation and the software applications used upon it should be compared in the following terms.

1. The total value of transactions, including movements in value of assets, processed over a given period. (Higher priority, given the usual scarce computer audit resources, should normally be given to higher values.)
2. The number of important accounts balances or other management information totals affected by the system. (A major system that handles

purchases, stock balances, losses, damages and produces year-end figures for current assets is likely to be more crucial in terms of fraud and corruption than a system that records and updates employees' training and qualifications records, though of course the latter will have some data protection and human resource management implications.)

3. The total number of transactions processed over a given period. (If, say, all but a few large commercial rental transactions relate to hundreds of peppercorn values of way-leaves, the few large ones can be isolated and quickly verified.)

4. The handling of personal data, especially any data of a sensitive nature relating to, say, income, illness or debt recovery. (Apart from the risk of prosecution under the Data Protection Act, employees, contractors or suppliers may be blackmailed by others or tempted to access and amend their own records if these are not protected.)

5. The political sensitivity of transactions in relation to known or anticipated areas of controversy such as repair times on empty properties, hospital waiting lists or funding of military research programmes. (This may have little direct practical effect in terms of fraud and corruption though politicians may be motivated to massage figures, with wider fraudulent consequences resulting.)

Such a loss and sensitivity assessment could, of course, be undertaken irrespective of the degree of computerization. In fact such considerations tend to be in the mind of any auditor undertaking an assignment. But, when applied to computer systems and to the allocation of management effort in planning, organizing and controlling computer installations and running the necessary applications, the five points above prove useful in minimizing the risk, and maximizing the likely detection of fraud and corruption.

Key controls review

The important systems identified from risk and sensitivity assessment are likely to vary from a laptop with software that records data relating to AIDS cases at hospitals, to a mainframe installation dedicated to the processing of a common payroll for several government departments or agencies. Commonly recurring questions of control are listed below. In practice every installation and software application will require individual attention.

1. Are control totals produced and independently reconciled to ensure the completeness, accuracy and correct disclosure (accountability) of transactions processed between initial input and final output; for example,

between manually produced timesheet totals by value and number and hourly paid wages payroll; or between changes in letting of domestic properties and weekly or monthly rent account totals?

2. Is a separation of duties maintained between staff who control the input of data (nowadays with increased PC use and networks these are often becoming the data user) and staff who act as programmers, software designers or systems maintainers and generally control the installation and the software? In a mainframe batch processing situation the operational and programming staff in particular should be separated including, if possible, physical separation of office accommodation.

3. Are any controls in place that independently verify input? Traditional bulk batch processing often involved all input data being separately keyed in and verified. If this is not feasible, are samples of input verified by supervisory or managerial staff?

4. Are controls in place to check access to the system, particularly while live data is being handled? Examples might include password controls, usually at different levels of authority, so that while junior officers can read files, only supervisors or a separate group of staff can enter transactions and only management can amend key fields such as debt redemption dates. Other access controls include, for example, physical measures such as high-security rooms, or key-operated switches on terminals.

5. Is a separation (mentioned in 2.) maintained at times of system changes or malfunction computer staff may require access to live data, particularly to standing or near-permanent data such as addresses, account numbers, etc. Given that additional maintenance may be carried out on a regular basis it is not unknown for computer staff to have relatively frequent access to live files and for any separation in duty, often carefully set up by the user, to be in effect overridden by computer staff with subsequent risks to the integrity of the data.

6. Is all access (including failed attempts) and any consequent data amendment traceable to the responsible officer? This is often best maintained by ensuring that every officer who can gain access is issued with a genuinely confidential password and that the use of his or her password automatically records that officer's name or initials in a field which cannot be subsequently amended and is reproduced in any hard-copy computer activity log.

7. Are independent authorizations kept for any changes to software or key fields and key data? This is particularly important when changes to access permissions or amendments to standing data are authorized.

8. Are adequate back-up copies of all work, client accounts, etc. kept? The traditional 'grandfather-father-son' level of copies is adequate for most situations.

9. Are the physical security controls, particularly access to site, regularly reviewed by an independent security manager, auditor or equivalent?

Many so-called computer frauds result from conventional theft of data or high value printed output such as cheques.

10. Is all sensitive or high value printed output subject to control such as stock control records, transfer authorization and, where appropriate, shredding after use?

11. Are electronic funds and sensitive data transmissions authenticated? This might, for example, be achieved by subsequent telephone calls, automatic confirmation such as that used by automatic bank transfer systems or the use of passwords between recipient and sender.

12. Are controls set up to ensure all exception reports are actioned by appropriate managers or technical officers? It is particularly critical for obvious reasons to ensure that arrangements continue operating during sickness, holidays, etc.

For the sake of brevity and impact the author has limited this review section to the dozen points above. If any manager considers that systems judged of high priority in the first review are significantly deficient in any of the above he or she should consider taking urgent advice and action.

Assessment of key personnel

Recruitment, retention and career development measures can, depending upon the particular circumstances, play an important role in minimizing fraud and corruption. This is particularly true of computer professionals.

1. References should always be followed up, if necessary telephoning the referees to clear up any ambiguity. Organizations often wish to avoid acrimonious dismissal, particularly prosecution and any attendant publicity resulting from computer fraud. Some organizations have been accused of giving unwarranted and misleading references simply to ensure corrupt personnel leave with the minimum of fuss.

2. New and temporary staff should be prevented from gaining access to and control over high value data, the transfer of significant assets or sensitive information.

3. Officers should be made fully aware of where their IT duties begin and end including comprehensive and up-to-date desk instructions and work manuals.

4. All staff should be aware of their responsibilities under the Data Protection Act 1984.

5. All holidays should be taken. (Fraudsters are often reluctant to take leave and risk any replacement gaining access to their work.)

6. An agreed procedure for review of career and performance and for counselling employees should be maintained. Computerization can introduce
additional, often boring, routine into previously interesting work patterns
(although sometimes the reverse is true). Some positions involve little
more than minimal intervention by operating staff into an automated
procedure. Such circumstances can engender a feeling of achievement in
managing to beat the system. This may manifest itself in nothing more
serious than altering human work routines to enable a few hours' sleep
during a night shift or using a PC to play games. Or it may, by only a few
incremental steps, lead to malicious diversion of funds or theft of data.

The legal framework

In Chapter 1 the reader saw something of how the law defines and attempts
to make broad provision for fraud and corruption. Most of the statutes
predate widespread computerization but three important exceptions are
discussed below.

Computer Misuse Act 1990

For many years it was held that the ordinary civil and criminal law was
adequate to deal with computer crime, the basic characteristics of which do
not differ from non-computer crime. The main difference was not the crime
but the medium of its perpetration. The phenomena of computer hacking
and viruses appear to be the main developments that discredited this view.
Hacking refers to gaining unauthorized access to computer data, usually due
to lack of adequate control over telephone links or insecure network arrangements. Hackers appear to come from a wide range of backgrounds and
motivations and many appear to be young, well-educated and motivated in
part at least by the thrill of what was, until 1990, not generally considered
illegal even though it arguably amounted to a form of breaking and entering.

A computer virus is a programmed unauthorized alteration to the data
stored in the memory or backup storage. Usually it arrives via corrupted software that has been purchased or copied on to magnetic disc. Like an organic
virus it reproduces itself as programs are executed and magnetic media are
utilized for memory or storage functions. Perhaps its most worrying characteristic is the relative ease of transmission between organizations and sites.

Neither of these two basic phenomena appeared to be adequately covered by existing law. Indeed there are claimed to be other equally serious omissions, such as a lack of measures to combat international computer fraud and the lack of a precise definition of a computer.

Nevertheless as far as hacking is concerned the Computer Misuse Act attempts to legislate against unauthorized access to computers in section 1 (the basic offence) and section 2 (the aggravated offence) and against unauthorized modifications (the virus offence) in section 4. Section 3 contains a separately worded offence to take into account Scottish law. Appendix 5.1 contains the relevant sections.

Data Protection Act 1984

This is a curious but at times useful act. It is not a very long piece of legislation considering its far-reaching aims. The act is not primarily designed to deal with fraud and corruption. Rather it aims to ensure that personal data, that is, data relating to living individuals, is held accurately, securely, in a publicly accountable manner and is used only for intended and registered purposes.

In practice almost every organization that has computer-held records relating to names, addresses, diseases, insurance policies, job descriptions or literally any data from which it would be possible to identify an individual, should complete a lengthy registration document. The registration covers such matters as:

1. the purposes for which the data is held;
2. the types of data held;
3. the sources from which the data is obtained;
4. to whom the data will be disclosed;
5. any transfers of data abroad and other details.

A summary of each organization's registration(s) is given in the publicly available data protection register, held at main libraries and at the headquarters of the Data Protection Registrar in Cheshire.

The Act (Schedule 1) also lays down eight principles governing the collection, holding, use and dissemination of computer-held personal data. Most importantly, from our point of view, the act provides that data shall be held securely and used only for the legitimate registered purposes, though it must be said that purposes are often recorded, as least in the public register, in fairly broad terms. The principles are summarized in Figure 5.2.

Figure 5.2 (Reproduced with kind permission of the Data Protection Registrar.)

In general the act provides an additional, and sometimes unintended, layer of defence against corruption and fraud. Most public sector bodies are particularly sensitive to their statutory obligations and this act brings computer security and secure systems within those obligations.

Copyright, Designs and Patents Act 1988

This Act is relevant to issues of fraud and corruption in so far as computer-related fraud may well involve the illegal copying of computer software. This offence is sometimes rather glamorously referred to as software piracy. The 1988 act lays down that for copyright purposes software programs may be considered in the same way as literary works and illegal copying can be the subject of civil or criminal redress in the courts.

Illegal copying from, say, a hard disc supplied by a software company to the purchaser's own soft disc and thence to other discs, is likely to be far more costly for the copyright owner than illegal photocopies from the pages of a book or magazine. The cost of a single copy of a piece of software can run into thousands of pounds. By comparison few people are likely to copy an entire book. Several recent examples of legal action or cases settled out of court indicate that software suppliers are starting to find enforcement action is now well worth paying for.

Summary

Apart from the technology involved in its perpetration, computer fraud is very similar to any fraud. The technology is changing all the time. Even the key controls outlined above gain or lose a little relevance with each new development. Despite these shifting sands the importance of separating key duties, of maintaining controls over computer input, processing and output and of independent control of the development, support and maintenance of all systems remains paramount. The chapter so far has outlined these features and attempted to identify review issues including key controls that can be widely applied to any computerized systems. The legal framework, originally mentioned in Chapter 1, has been further considered as it pertains to computer-related security.

Case studies

The first case relates to armed robbery and blackmail. It illustrates the need for close control of sensitive personal data. The second case considers the security and access controls consistent with large mainframe computer facilities.

Case study 5.1 The Gallery Sports Club

Beneath the headquarters of a government department, located in a basement, is a social and sports club, the Gallery. Members are drawn from a wide spectrum of the civil service, national health service and other public services.

A computerized membership and booking system has recently been introduced. The system handles advance bookings from members and non-members, cash receipts at the reception area, invoicing of debtors, cancellations, and – the weak link in this case – membership records.

Membership costs £30.00 per annum plus additional rates for specialized activities including the gun club. A typical membership record gives wide-ranging details of name, address, next of kin, rank, workplace, including quite often work contact telephone numbers and a membership number to which is suffixed a letter to identify any special activities; G for gun club, Q for squash, C for cycling, etc.

The letter enabled each membership number to be used by the computer to calculate total annual fees owed and automatically invoice these to the member.

The entire system consisted of a small processor, a printer and three terminals, two at reception and one in the club secretary's office. Neither the secretary nor any other officials of the club including the four part-time receptionists had any previous experience of using a computerized system. The company that installed the hardware and provided the software did an adequate job of instructing their customer in using the system, but little if any guidance was provided in ensuring adequate security. The shortcomings in internal control and the contravention of the Data Protection Act (of which the staff were unaware) only came to light when a wave of gun thefts took place.

As is usual in such cases the benefit of hindsight revealed a complete lack of computer security. Like so many small PC and network systems operated by relatively inexperienced staff the following were among the serious inadequacies.

1. Inadequate password control over access. A single password was used to access the entire system, usually at the start of each day. It was normal practice to leave the terminal in the secretary's office switched on throughout the day irrespective of who was in the room at the time. The password had in any case not been changed since the system was installed and was widely known to staff and some members of the organizing committee of the club. Ideally passwords should be changed every few weeks.

2. No one was aware of the need to register the system with the Data Protection Registrar (exemptions might apply to private clubs but not in this case) or to operate the system in compliance with the principles set out in the Data Protection Act.

3. Control over output on screen or printouts was negligible. Summary printouts of members, fees outstanding, change of address details, etc. were held in ring binders on open shelves either behind the reception desk or in the secretary's office. Both these locations were subject to access by members with enquiries and to sales people. Screens were frequently left switched on and unattended.

4. No facility was available for any of the screens to be 'blanked' without the user having to exit from the enquiry facility he or she was currently using. Thus customers or other visitors were often left alone with a live screen while the receptionist or the secretary went to obtain information or was called away to deal with an enquiry.

In this case it came as no surprise to the investigating police and senior civil service management that a printout of members' addresses with G suffixes (about 14 in all) had found its way into the hands of a criminal/terrorist gang who had raided most of the addresses on the night of the annual Sports Club dinner. Most properties were empty at the time but several members and their families had been tied up and gagged and one had been shot and wounded. During this one evening about 20 weapons had been stolen.

In addition to the theft of data relating to weapons, investigations revealed that the club had regularly disclosed membership lists (without suffixes) to a company selling sports goods. There was no risk of fraud here but given the failure to notify members of the intention to disclose this information or to register the disclosure with the Data Protection Registrar it was nevertheless an infringement of the law.

Obvious lessons emerge from this case. The general attitude towards computerization and internal control was extremely lax. Access controls, control over output and a general attitude of care for and compliance with the law relating to personal data are obviously required.

In practice screens in an area visible to the public should be capable of being blanked, and operators should log off from the system when screens are not in use. Passwords should be reviewed regularly. Output should be stored in a secure manner. In this case a thief could have generated the list, stolen a copy already printed, hand or photocopied a list or even noted the details from a screen left unattended.

In respect of the Data Protection Act it is worth noting that where serious non-compliance occurs individuals as well as organizations may be the subject of legal action.

Case study 5.2 Central Health Authority mainframe installation

The Central Regional Health Authority operates a major mainframe computer installation which offers its services directly to independent trust hospitals, districts and other health service bodies.

Various applications are run on the mainframe which has since the introduction of competitive marketing in the health service proved a popular facility. Two large mainframes are operated and a separate local area network advisory service (LANADS) is available to users at an annual subscription. *Ad hoc* consultancy projects are also undertaken.

A recent report by the external auditor has pointed out that the current staffing levels are considerably higher than similar ones elsewhere. Management do not dispute the auditor's findings but point out that while the computer unit are managing to cover all their costs from recharges they are reluctant to make staff redundant. Natural wastage will, they anticipate, enable staff numbers to be reduced. They also intend retraining some staff to cope with the small but growing advice and consultancy service offered to outside bodies.

At about the same time as the external auditor's report an internal auditor's report pointed out that the log of computer operations was likely to be inaccurate and was in any case incomplete for about a quarter of the past year. The same report also pointed out that formal authorizations of 'change-control' procedures were unacceptable (authorization sheets were generally unsigned and the reasons given for a program change were too short to be meaningful). Copy programs and systems documentation, especially security copies, were not updated on a regular basis and exception reports had no evidence of any review or action taken (though on this point the computer manager insisted that actions were taken but agreed they were not adequately documented).

During a meeting between the internal auditor and the computer manager the latter accepted the main points of the report. The auditor also raised several agreed points arising from the previous year's reports that were still to be implemented relating to physical security as follows.

1. Physical access to the computer. A main corridor, lift and stairs used by all staff at central headquarters runs through the suite. The doors to the main computer room though lockable are frequently left unlocked as staff need to pass between the mainframes and the control areas. Smoke detectors are in place but these use an old-fashioned sprinkler system which if set off accidentally or maliciously would cause immense damage compared to modern gas-based extinguishers.
2. Magnetic storage is on site rendering it vulnerable in the event of disaster.
3. Emergency back-up procedures in the event of accidental or malicious disaster have not been tested for several years and appear out of date.
4. The windows are of normal glass and though kept locked are considered unlikely to present an acceptable level of deterrence. The computer suite contains several million pounds worth of movable hardware (excluding the mainframes) and is located on the ground floor.

These points have been re-addressed by the external auditor in his reports.

The staff association has asked that computer staff receive a special market premium in addition to the annual negotiated pay settlement. They point out that staff turnover is relatively high and pay rates lower than several published surveys. Morale, they say, is generally low.

In this particular scenario it is quite likely that the management and auditors would have continued to make faltering progress towards improving security and internal controls. Extra security costs money. Staff morale is already likely to be poor given the turnover and any extra red tape such as adequate descriptions and authorization of changes to programs set out in change-control authorization is likely to be treated with resistance if not contempt. The computer staff probably realize the site is overstaffed. For some posts boredom and the lack of challenge or job satisfaction may be an additional demoralizing influence.

In such a situation a major event can often act as a catalyst to improvement. Ideally this might be a complete change in senior management or in management attitudes, introducing an ethos of greater professionalism, an ethos that encourages higher standards, if only perhaps because these are felt to be worth achieving for their own sake, despite the apparent acceptance of the current service quality by the users. If a new management outlook is not forthcoming then at least a more persuasive and hard-hitting audit approach might encourage managers to rectify the current problems before disaster strikes. In this case, not unusually perhaps, disaster struck first. It came in the form of a major fraud involving unauthorized use of computing resources by staff to develop private software and the embarrassing release of sensitive personal health data.

A senior programmer who had been forced to resign from her previous employment for perpetrating a similar offence on a lesser scale could not resist the temptation to start up in business a second time. No legal or disciplinary action had been taken by her previous employers, an insurance company, who had in fact provided a short and acceptable reference. During interview the lady explained that she had left her previous employer to live close to her sick mother. Given her outstanding qualifications, no further queries were considered necessary.

Compared to her previous employment she found her new workload less demanding and the controls, especially the log of computer usage and controls over the testing of new or amended programs, were lax. Her illegal activities and those of her close colleagues to whom her corrupting influence had spread, might have continued unnoticed. However some of the test data used to illustrate the functions of the software being developed and sold contained, unintentionally, live records of recent patient treatment. One of these records was found, to the annoyance of its subject, to have been purchased by himself from a small independent company set up by the perpetrators to market their illicitly produced software. The subject complained to the Health Authority. His complaint was found to be well founded and he was awarded considerable compensation. The perpetrators were quickly dismissed, this time with considerable publicity. A great deal more public money was spent recovering patient records and compensating firms who had purchased the illegal software.

The main lesson from this case is of course that such a situation should not have been allowed to arise in the first place, but more than this, that we should look beyond technical issues of internal control, physical security, etc. to the underlying corporate attitudes in attempting to understand the wider causes and risk. In particular new staff should be screened and existing staff (who were soon dragged into this case) must not be taken for granted. Regular performance review by senior management, as suggested by the staff themselves, and career development counselling might well have revealed a bored and disgruntled workforce with a high level of unsatisfied skills and the opportunity and temptation to use these to ill effect.

Concluding points

This chapter has considered 'ordinary' fraud and corruption in relation to information technology. A computerized working environment has become a feature of most public sector bodies. Certain familiar aspects of fraud and corruption and the appropriate countermeasures must be seen afresh.

Protection and control of physical assets and access to computer hardware; accounting for changes in program software and in key data; separation of duties; confidentiality of financial or personal data and password control – these are just a few of the important issues.

Certain standard procedures take on an added significance in relation to information technology, particularly in relation to staff recruitment.

The second case study illustrates the importance of independent audit and an independent and detached frame of mind when dealing with or managing information technology. It is often worthwhile to turn one's mind away from the demands of ever-changing technological details to what appear to be the overall objectives of the computerized system. These objectives should be those of the people who control and operate the system, and of the organizations of which it is part. If they are not and, say, objectives of individual line management are out of synchronization with corporate objectives or the intended use of the system and this has been allowed to persist, then there is every chance that assets might be used corruptly and fraud occur without detection.

Usually the objectives of anyone, especially the auditor, wishing to prevent fraud will coincide with sound management provided such objectives are not taken to the extreme. Given the rapidly changing pace of new computer technology more trust than usual may need to be placed in the technical experts especially when new systems are being introduced. In many ways this means that all the more weight should be given to ensuring that key controls such as those described in this chapter are introduced, and introduced effectively. Such controls should be designed to meet as many as possible of the following objectives.

1. To ensure the new technology satisfies a genuine need in line with political policy, corporate strategy and management objectives.
2. To ensure technology is acquired and used honestly, economically, efficiently and effectively, i.e. offers fraud-free 'VFM'.
3. To ensure the accuracy, fairness and relevance of the financial and management information produced by each system.
4. To ensure the adequacy and on-going reliability of each system as a whole and all its controls (in line with 1, 2, and 3 above).

These objectives may apply, of course, to any non-computerized system and are, depending on the circumstances, likely to be interdependent.

A frame of mind that keeps in view these objectives often requires that the computer auditor should not consider himself as 'auditing the computer' or the manager as 'managing the computer'. Rather they should consider themselves as auditing or managing a part of the system for maximizing the return from land and buildings, or processing salaries and wages, or ensuring a defence need is maintained, depending upon the audit or corporate objectives that apply to them. Given the need to keep up with technology attaining such a frame of mind can present the manager or auditor with a genuine professional challenge.

Appendix 5.1   Extract from the Computer Misuse Act 1990 (S1 to S4)*

SECTION 1

THE BASIC OFFENCE

1. (1) A person is guilty of an offence if –
   (a) he causes a computer to perform any function with intent to secure access to any program or data held in any computer;
   (b) the access he intends to secure is unauthorised; and
   (c) he knows at the time when he causes the computer to perform the function that that is the case.

   (2) The intent a person has to have to commit an offence under this section need not be directed at –
   (a) any particular program or data;
   (b) a program or data of any particular kind; or
   (c) a program or data held in any particular computer.

   (3) A person guilty of an offence under this section shall be liable on summary conviction to imprisonment for a term not exceeding six months or to a fine not exceeding level 5 on the standard scale or to both.

SECTION 2

THE AGGRAVATED OFFENCE

2. (1) A person is guilty of an offence under this section if he commits an offence under section 1 above ('the unauthorised access offence') with intent –
   (a) to commit an offence to which this section applies; or
   (b) to facilitate the commission of such an offence (whether by himself or by any other person);
   and the offence he intends to commit or facilitate is referred to below in this section as the further offence.

   (2) This section applies to offences –
   (a) for which the sentence is fixed by law; or

---

* Only the minimal description of the offences are contained in this appendix. The act itself, particularly S 18, should be referred to for any detailed interpretation.

(b) for which a person of twenty-one years of age or over (not previously convicted) may be sentenced to imprisonment for a term of five years (or might be so sentenced but for the restrictions imposed by section 33 of the Magistrates' Courts Act 1990).

(3) It is immaterial for the purposes of this section whether the further offence is to be committed on the same occasion as the unauthorised access offence or on any future occasion.

(4) A person may be guilty of an offence under this section even though the facts are such that the commission of the further offence is impossible.

(5) A person guilty of an offence under this section shall be liable –
   (a) on summary conviction, to imprisonment for a term not exceeding six months or to a fine not exceeding the statutory maximum or to both; and
   (b) on conviction on indictment, to imprisonment for a term not exceeding five years or to a fine or to both.

(6) This section does not extend to Scotland.

SECTION 3

THE SCOTS' OFFENCE

3. (1) A person is guilty of an offence under this section if he commits an offence under section 1 above ('the unauthorised access offence') with intent –
   (a) to obtain a significant personal or material advantage for himself or another person; or
   (b) to damage seriously another person's interests.

(2) A person may be guilty of an offence under this section even though the facts are such that it is impossible for him to carry out his intent.

(3) A person guilty of an offence under this section shall be liable –
   (a) on summary conviction, to imprisonment for a term not exceeding six months or to a fine not exceeding the statutory maximum or to both; and
   (b) on conviction on indictment, to imprisonment for a term not exceeding five years or to a fine or to both.

(4) This section extends to Scotland only.

SECTION 4

THE VIRUS OFFENCE

4. (1) A person is guilty of an offence if –
   (a) he does any act which causes an unauthorised modification of the contents of any computer's memory or of the contents of any other computer storage medium; and
   (b) at the time when he does the act he has the requisite intent and the requisite knowledge.

   (2) For the purpose of subsection (1)(b) above the requisite intent is an intent to cause a modification of the contents of any computer's memory or of the contents of any such medium and by so doing –
   (a) to impair the operation of any computer or of any computer program; or
   (b) to destroy or impair the reliability or accessibility of any data stored or otherwise held in any computer's memory or stored on or in any such medium.
   (c) any particular modification or a modification of any particular kind.

   (4) For the purposes of subsection (1)(b) above the requisite knowledge is knowledge that any modification he intends to cause is unauthorised.

   (5) It is immaterial for the purposes of this section whether an unauthorised modification is permanent or merely temporary.

   (6) A person guilty of an offence under this section shall be liable –
   (a) on summary conviction, to imprisonment for a term not exceeding six months or to a fine not exceeding the statutory maximum or to both; and
   (b) on conviction on indictment, to imprisonment for a term not exceeding five years or to a fine or to both.

6

Revenue expenditure systems

Introduction

The systems that facilitate revenue expenditure on goods and services – broadly speaking, sundry creditors' payments and their associated activities – deserve special attention. Individual payments may often be of relatively low value compared to capital payments discussed in Chapter 4 but there is strong evidence that the revenue expenditure systems are among the most frequently abused and, in total, account for more fraud than most other systems. The only convenient published public sector statistics come from the Audit Commission. For reported frauds over £500 the Commission's published figures show that over six years from 1983/84 to 1990/91, of £11 m worth of frauds nearly £3.5 m, just under a third, related to 'creditor payments' (see Further reading). In fact such statistics are likely to seriously underestimate both the total value of 'creditors' system frauds and indeed total frauds. Many frauds are, individually, likely to be for smaller amounts than the £500 and, of course, a great many frauds go unreported and probably very many more go undetected. Indications of unreported fraud from other sources, such as the Home Office and various crime statistics, vary widely but even conservative extrapolations for all (private and public sector) frauds are in figures of over £3 bn. See for example Levi in the Further reading section. The level of fraud detected in the public sector is far lower than in the private sector, but whether or not this is due mainly to greater honesty and less opportunity in the public sector (as the writer would like to believe) is left to the reader's judgement.

Whatever the correct statistics which no one will ever know for certain, creditor payments is a critical area for fraud prevention. A serious level of fraud discovered among the expenditure systems is often indicative of more widespread malaise and corruption. Sometimes frauds can be shown to arise solely in unusual circumstances or isolated locations. But, in general, only a few cases of revenue expenditure fraud will indicate serious internal control problems.

A trail of responsibility

An 'audit trail' or trail of responsibility should exist throughout the revenue expenditure systems, as shown in Figure 6.1. This trail should be able to demonstrate:

1. who required a purchase to be made and for what purpose;
2. who ordered it and if possible at what estimated cost;
3. who checked it was satisfactorily received (or performed in the case of services); and
4. who authorized payment to be made.

At each stage from ordering, through receipt of goods and invoice to actual payment, separate records of the individual quantities and values involved should be kept.

Ideally, the main duties involved, i.e.

1. ordering and buying
2. custody and usage
3. book-keeping and recording and
4. final distribution of any cheques, etc.

should as far as possible be undertaken by separate officers. At times, particularly in smaller organizations or local offices, complete separation of duties may prove too costly to be efficient. Even in larger organizations officers may be unavailable when an urgent need is established or an urgent payment is required. In these circumstances, at least two separate officers should be actively involved in the payment authorization prior to payment being despatched (whether payment is by post, electronic funds transfer, or even by handing over cash to a supplier).

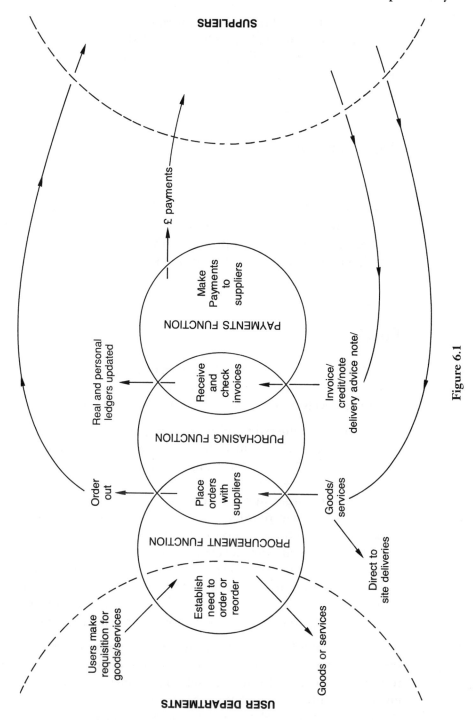

SUPPLIERS

3 payments

Make
Payments
to
suppliers

PAYMENTS FUNCTION

Real and personal
ledgers updated

Receive
and check
invoices

Invoice/
credit/note
delivery advice note/

PURCHASING FUNCTION

Order
out

Place
orders
with
suppliers

Goods/
services

PROCUREMENT FUNCTION

Direct to
site deliveries

Establish
need to
order or
reorder

Users make
requisition for
goods/services

Goods or services

USER DEPARTMENTS

Figure 6.1

An acceptable level of internal controls in a typical organization's revenue expenditure system would involve most of the following (or a high level of compensating, and usually costly, control activity such as direct supervision by senior management).

Procurement

Official requisition forms that are:

1. prenumbered with a record of all spoils or cancelled forms and the officer responsible for controlling forms Nos 1... to... n;
2. signed and dated by the officer(s) authorized to requisition goods/services and, if different, the officer requiring the goods/services.

Purchasing

The above will usually suffice for internal requisitions, e.g. for goods already purchased and held in store. For external purchases, whether required to top up reorder levels or for *ad hoc* items control would normally include:

3. Official prenumbered purchase orders (possibly using the same form as for internal requisition as in 1 above) also signed and dated by an authorized officer as for 2 above. Most importantly, a separation of duties should be maintained between the officer requiring the goods or services who initiated the order in the first place (or is responsible for confirming the need for regular reorders) and the officer undertaking the buying or purchasing of goods or services for the organization.
4. Delegated expenditure levels for individual ordering officers, or budget holders, or whoever is responsible for finally authorizing the purchase. Where, as is often the case, a central buying officer makes all purchases on behalf of numerous ordering officers these should have delegated expenditure levels set and made known to the buying officer.

If 3 and 4 are not feasible, possibly due to manpower budget restrictions or to the small size of the organization, a senior finance officer (or whoever is responsible for monitoring expenditure against budgets but is not directly involved in initiating purchases) should check all purchase documentation or at least a judgmental selection, depending on time available, to ensure:

(a) goods or services do not appear *ultra vires*, i.e. beyond the statutory powers of the public body;
(b) the quantity and nature appear reasonable in relation to the ordering officer's duties;
(c) the order has been properly completed and signed and dated by an officer authorized so to do;
(d) any delegated expenditure levels (per item or per budget ceiling) are not exceeded.

If possible any major physical assets should be verified by inspection.

Delivery

This is often the most difficult stage over which to maintain reliable control. Goods can arrive at various, often unexpected, locations sometimes direct to a building site or perhaps to a remote sub-office. The carrier is often in a great hurry to get on with the next delivery and may not even be clearly aware of the nature of the goods he is unloading. The 'delivery' of services is often impossible to fully verify. Goods can at least be counted or measured but who is to say that a service engineer has accurately and diligently checked a piece of equipment, or that a professional legal opinion has been based on careful judgement? If such services are inadequate this will usually be revealed in time but not until long after payment has been made and little hope of recovery remains.

Despite these difficulties some of the more useful controls are given below.

5. Delivery advice notes for goods should be signed by the consignor or on his behalf by the carrier and by the consignee, preferably after the latter has checked the delivery. The author has yet to come across large deliveries of bricks being individually counted or reels of wire being measured before the carrier has left the site but should any queries arise once the materials have been checked an unsigned delivery note can cause problems. It is generally acceptable practice for the site foreman, storekeeper, night security officer or whoever accepts a delivery to sign 'for receipt only' or 'accepted not checked'. This is done on the understanding that undue delay would be entailed in checking at the time and place of delivery and a reputable supplier would take the word of a reputable customer on the odd occasion a discrepancy arises. Notwithstanding these obvious exceptions most goods can be checked and signed for without undue effort before the delivery advice note is signed.

Very occasionally firms will deliver without an advice note. In such circumstances a photocopy order also signed, or a separate 'in-house' goods received note must be made up.

6. The delivery advice or goods received note should be matched to the order and the order marked off. Again, this should if possible be done prior to the departure of the carrier. It is surprising how often invoices are subsequently matched to orders and paid while the delivery advice note is ignored. Often handwritten adjustments or only part deliveries are noted on the advice note but this information takes time to get back to the supplier's accounts payable department, who invoice on the assumption that full payment is owed. If the consignee has paid an invoice against an order that has not been matched and annotated to show any discrepancy, any attempt to chase up late delivery of goods still outstanding (that may have been paid for) is likely to run into severe delays. This problem may be lessened when combined delivery note/invoices are used by suppliers but only if the purchase orders are carefully matched to delivery prior to payment.

Payment authorization

This is, or should be, the stage at which evidence from all the foregoing stages are drawn together.

7. Each payment should be separately authorized. This statement seems fairly straightforward, though in fact several complications can arise. Varying methods of payment must all be subject to a common standard of authorization, e.g.
   (a) cash;
   (b) computer-produced cheque runs;
   (c) *ad hoc* cheque payment;
   (d) automatic bank transfers;
   (e) credit notes issued;
   (f) payable orders issued by HM Paymaster General.

In any one organization several main methods are likely to be used; regular cheque runs and bank transfers are very common. Throughout, central government payable orders issued by HM Paymaster General are commonly used. Other media affecting payment or transferring credit may be used but a common standard should ensure the following.

8. Whatever method of final authorization for payment is used (signature, official seal/stamp, computer password/code) the authorizing officer

should have been able to examine evidence usually in the form of a subordinate's certification upon the invoice showing:

(a) that (the goods or services were ordered and the order was crossed off cancelled/marked as part-delivered or otherwise annotated to show the goods/services delivered were in fact required. Apart from ensuring an important defence against fraud this control ensures an excessive or even misdelivered consignment is spotted before payment. It is useful in ensuring no duplicate payments occur. Many firms will re-invoice if payment has not been promptly received. Suppliers commonly telephone organizations to speed up payment. If the person they speak to does not have their invoice conveniently to hand, another or a copy is quite likely to be hastily despatched. Unless the invoice is compared to an order which has to be annotated (or all invoices are dealt with by only one clerk with an infallible memory) there is a very high probability of two invoices going through the system and resulting in duplicate payment.

(b) that the goods or services were adequate;

(c) that the prices charges were as agreed or as advertised;

(d) that the arithmetic, (including VAT, cost centre code, etc.) has been checked;

(e) that any other specific requirements of the body have been performed such as dual authorization of amounts over a certain value.

Points (a) to (e) above are fairly standard for most organizations. In any large organization several different officers are likely to be involved and each should sign to confirm the stage(s) he or she has performed. This will evidence a trail of responsibility. Wherever this paper trail disappears into a computerized system the person(s) responsible for processing payments, or confirming that their part of stages (a) to (e) has been completed, must be able to evidence their authorization in a secure manner. In this respect secure password control is essential.

When only one person has responsibility for authorizing a particular computerized stage the part of the system affected must be protected by a password unique to that person. However, when more than one person can have responsibility for authorizing a particular stage, for example checking goods received or checking the arithmetic of the invoice, then secure authorization becomes more difficult.

In such circumstances each operator must be able to generate a unique password. Once the system has been accessed, using this unique password, evidence should remain on screen and printout – without revealing the password – of which officer accessed and amended the data. For example each password once keyed in should automatically generate the initials or name of the password owner in a predesignated tamperproof field.

Unfortunately when several passwords are being used the chance of one becoming known to an unauthorized person is increased. Reasonably frequent password changes help, as do limitations on attempted system entry – points which were discussed in Chapter 5.

The complaint is sometimes raised that evidence that points (a) to (e) above have been certified prior to final authorization will mean 'mountains of paperwork' for the manager to wade through before signing the authorization or pressing the keyboard. This, in fact, would only be a real problem in a poorly managed system. The authorizing officer would normally be expected to rely on the signatures present on one summary document. This usually means the supplier's invoice must be forwarded to each relevant officer controlling stages (a) to (e) usually with a 'grid' stamped clearly on the front or (less securely) an authorization slip stapled to it.

Payment production and distribution

The final part of the payment stage is yet to come and this is the part most often ignored by management once they have completed their authorization.

9. Controls should exist to ensure that what has been authorized – and only what has been authorized – is paid. A cheque run, sometimes involving the production of thousands of computer-printed and presigned cheques, will usually be produced. Electronic and automatic funds transfer from the organization's own to possibly thousands of recipient bank accounts via 'BACS', 'CHAPS', 'GIRO' or similar arrangements are also common. Superimposed on these procedures will be urgent, usually manually produced, cheques and sometimes even large cash disbursements. Some of the more common controls are as follows.
    (a) Separate (manual) validation of input is still used in many batch input systems. Though this method of inputting information to the computer is becoming less and less efficient in the face of on-line updating it is often maintained simply because it works and the immediate risks and costs of change are perceived as high. Usually a batch 'header' slip is initialled by the officer who verified it. A single batch may consist of hundreds of payments though most batches are smaller.
        A wide range of computer controls are discussed in Chapter 5. But manual procedures may still have a key part to play.
    (b) At some point an overall reconciliation must take place. Usually this takes place in a central creditors section but it may be performed by devolved budget holders. The key question to ask is: 'Has the

computerized payments system done what it was 'told' to do?' Computer managers will usually say 'Of course. The system can only do what it was told to do.' But all too often by 'system' they simply mean the hardware or at most the hardware and software. Hardware can malfunction, software can be poorly or corruptly designed or altered and both hardware and software are only as good as the people operating them. Where batch inputting is used payment schedules will usually be made up, perhaps for the whole organization, perhaps by division or section. Output reports should be available with payment totals that can be reconciled to the input schedules. Ideally this task should be undertaken by an officer not involved in the payment system up to this point, otherwise it should be undertaken by the budget holder or the officer making up the payment schedules. For a devolved on-line creditor payments systems, where no schedule or batches are prepared, the budget holder, who may indeed be the authorizing officer, should be in a position to reconcile output. A cheque production run will normally take place no more frequently than weekly or at most daily and printouts or screen displays should be made immediately available to the officer responsible for reconciliation. It is important to realize that many 'exception' reports made available by systems that carry out automatic reconciliations from input to output are rarely sufficient to deter fraud. Automatic reconciliation invariably depends upon the input being correct and untampered with in the first place and then being adequately vetted by processing controls within the system software. A miskeyed amount, fraudulent amounts entered while terminals are left unattended or amounts produced by software that has been 'bugged' are unlikely to come to light through exception reporting.

10. As part of the final procedures of payment systems within most organizations come controls (if any) over posting out. Post rooms can be the scene of frantic activity towards the end of the working day but as a general rule someone must find time to take responsibility for counting and agreeing the number of creditor payments to be posted out. These should be signed for on transfer between cheque production (and possibly enveloping) and transfer to post room. Even if these duties are all undertaken immediately after cheque production it is still valid for the number of payments to be counted. The number of individual payments posted should be agreed to the cheque production run – usually a single figure at the end of a printout. For automatic bank transfer payment statements should be received from the banks to confirm the completeness of receipt of a transmission or the completeness of receipt of payments processed on tape or other magnetic media. These statements should include total debits and credits by value and number,

which should be agreed to in-house payment listings or be forwarded to budget holders and authorizing officers to be agreed in the same way as cheque runs.

11. Ideally, the distribution procedures, especially for cheques and payable orders, etc. should not 'backtrack', i.e. involve officers who have initiated or certified any stage or finally authorized payment. Thus if a false payment is generated it must be 'forced out' of the organization. The perpetrator of a fraud would then need a false address, or risk using his own address at which to collect the cheque or similar. Otherwise it is a simple matter for him or her to take possession of the cheque as it comes back into the system. Any exception to this rule, such as cheques that have to be handed over personally, during perhaps an exchange of legal documents, should be clearly sanctioned by senior managers.

This is a convenient point to summarize the key areas of internal control in the basic procurement–purchase–payment system.

1. Prenumbered and signed authorization for requisition and ordering.
2. Delegated expenditure levels and budgeting control.
3. Separation of duties.
4. Matching of deliveries to orders and marking the latter as received.
5. Separate authorization of each payment.
6. An identifiable chain of certifying officers responsible for checking each payment, culminating in the final authorization of payment.
7. Reconciliation of input of payments by value and number to output totals of cheques, etc. produced.
8. Agreement of cheques produced to cheques posted out.
9. No 'backtracking' of payment.

Case studies

Two case studies follow. The first is very brief but typical of an increasing problem.

The relatively high risk of fraud in a poorly controlled expenditure system is generally recognized. As was mentioned at the start of the chapter this is an area particularly prone to fraud. No system can give complete assurance against deliberate and planned fraud especially if collusion occurs. The rewards of a successful fraud in this area can often be very large and tend to involve an element of recurrence. This means, as will be illustrated in the second case, that dishonest officers may be prepared to accept an element of risk that in other systems might act as a deterrent and that once a method of perpetration has been devised it will be tried over and over again. Similar features of high risk/high reward apply to capital works payments discussed in Chapter 4.

Case study 6.1 The Public Organizations Directory Exchange (PODE)

PODE is a fictitious example of a false billing organization. The usual aim of false billing agencies is to obtain a large number of relatively small payments from as many organizations as possible who are, most importantly, a safe distance beyond realistic recovery action. They rely on poor internal controls in the organization targeted on appearing credible at first sight. For example:

1. they have names and logos similar in sound, spelling and appearance to genuine suppliers;
2. their services are difficult to validate in a tangible manner and the goods will have been consumed, processed or passed on prior to the arrival of their invoice;
3. their bills are timed to arrive when workloads are high but budgets are largely unspent; when regular officers are likely to be on leave; when calls to outside bodies often go unanswered. Late December is a favourite 'targeting' time.

The PODE was set up in Zurich using a post box address. It distributed invoices for inclusion in various so-called 'international directories'. Typically, no sales promotional literature accompanied the invoice which was usually phrased in terms of renewal of an existing subscription. This avoided placing the officer(s) on whose desk the invoice eventually landed in the position of having to decide if the 'service' offered was actually worth having. Someone it seemed had already set the precedent last year, or the year before perhaps. The amounts involved were usually small – under £50 or £100 – as many relatively junior budget holders have limits set at such levels, and invariably described as overdue or subject to prompt payment discount if paid within a few days of the estimated receipt by the target body.

It is very difficult for the payee organization to prove one way or another whether the directory actually existed. No copies are ever sent out. Though, no doubt, if the perpetrators behind PODE were ever forced into court a listing of some sort would be produced. In the meantime the officer(s) authorizing payment could well be expected to forget the matter or assume that a directory had been sent to the legal or perhaps the public relations departments. Figure 6.2 gives an example of PODE invoices.

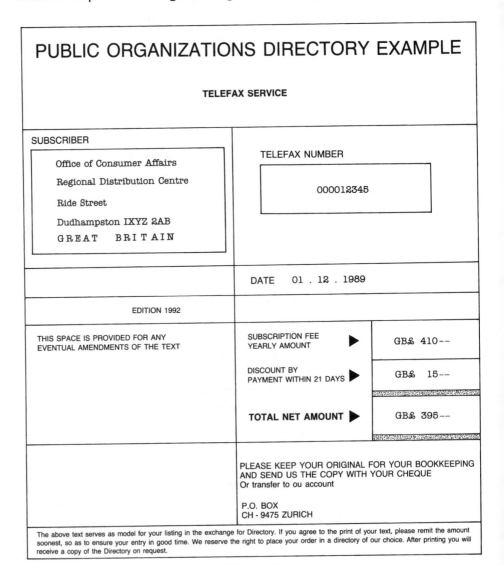

Figure 6.2

Case study 6.2   Greater Harmborough Council

This authority has been formed by the expansion of the old Harmborough City Council into its rural hinterland swallowing up large parts of neighbouring rural districts to form a single unitary authority.

Greater Harmborough already operates a centralized purchasing system. On to this system has been grafted the purchasing arrangements for a housing area local office inherited from one of the disbanded districts.

The housing area local office (HALO) is one of five decentralized offices based among the larger estates owned by the new council. The other four were part of the original city council. HALOs allocate properties to families on the waiting list, make rent collections and authorize routine jobbing, i.e. day-to-day repairs. Each HALO has its own budget allocations.

The deputy director of housing has been concerned at the past three monthly expenditure returns of the new HALO that almost 70% of its annual budget allocation has been spent by the end of the first quarter. The area housing manager in charge of the new HALO has explained that the former authority had been far more generous in its allocation and his staff were finding it difficult to adapt to Harmborough's more stringent regime. This issue has become a source of growing conflict between the director and the area manager, to the extent that the latter has hinted he may resign if more funds are not forthcoming. Most of the overspend relates to jobbing repairs contracted out by the HALO, either to the DSO or local firms, on a 'craft' basis each year. Currently the DSO craftsmen have won the contract for non-emergency plumbing and electrical work while all emergency repairs, carpentry, bricklaying and other trades are undertaken by local tradesmen and builders. The director's suspicions of fraud are aroused when a property condition survey undertaken by his staff reveals that the new HALO's property is in an abysmal state of repair compared to the other four HALOs despite all the extra expenditure. Also, some streets mentioned by the area manager as having been the recipients of many jobbing repairs to gutters, roof tiles, and windows appear to be in the worst state of disrepair according to the survey. The director approaches the chief internal auditor. A routine evaluation of the systems for undertaking jobbing repairs is carried out. Figure 6.3 gives a flow chart summary. Key controls questions are:

1. Are all repairs needed by genuine tenants?
2. Are all repairs correctly assessed, e.g. as emergency, non-urgent?
3. Are all repairs carried out adequately and at the right time?
4. Are all repairs (i.e. by job) correctly costed and coded? (Labour plus materials plus any other cost or agreed charges.)

In the case of the new HALO a serious control weakness was identified (as shown on Figure 6.3). The independent confirmation of the work was totally inadequate.

Very few pre-inspections were undertaken and post-inspection was limited to about 50% of jobs that were, effectively, selected by a receptionist.

Tenants would telephone or call into the HALO which employed one full-time receptionist who, although she might not receive all the incoming calls or visitors, was usually called upon to deal with repair enquiries. Over several years she had built up expertise in the relatively complex task of summarizing the tenants' description of damages and the necessary action to be taken plus likely materials needed. These details were entered directly on to a job sheet and classified by the receptionist as emergency, high priority or low priority depending on the nature of the damage. Virtually no guidance was available defining the types of work to be put into each category which was left to the discretion of the receptionist and the vociferousness of the tenant. If the receptionist was on leave a building inspector was normally called upon to deal with repair enquiries.

The receptionist was able to accept bribes from local firms and tradesmen to:

1. make out false job sheets for work that had not been requested. Later the invoice would be matched to the job sheet by a clerk in the finance department and paid provided the receptionist had stamped 'passed for payment' on the job sheet.
2. classify genuine work that was medium or low priority as emergency repairs for which a higher rate per hour was paid;
3. exaggerate the amount of work required on a genuine job.

She also accepted bribes from desperate tenants.

The job sheets were not sequentially prenumbered and the receptionist was trusted by the building works inspectors employed by the architects' department to send them undercopies of all job sheets. The inspectors were under the false impression that they pre-inspected all non-emergency work and post-inspected all jobs.

The 'passed for payment' stamp used by the receptionist was intended to be kept and used only by the HALO manager and the building inspectors. This was strictly the case at all other HALOs but at the new HALO the manager had, in his previous authority, been in the habit of delegating his authority to authorize payment to his deputy and other officers, and the stamp to authorize payment was kept unlocked and freely accessible among other stamps for general use in the office.

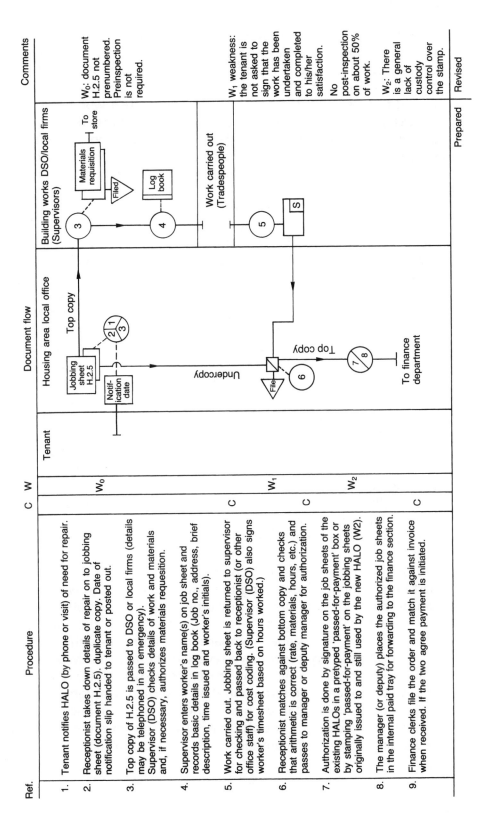

Figure 6.3

Ref.	C	W	Procedure	Comments
1.			Tenant notifies HALO (by phone or visit) of need for repair.	
2.		W_0	Receptionist takes down details of repair on to jobbing sheet (document H.2.5). duplicate copy. Date of notification slip handed to tenant or posted out.	W_0: document H.2.5 not prenumbered. Preinspection is not required.
3.			Top copy of H.2.5 is passed to DSO or local firms (details may be telephoned in an emergency). Supervisor (DSO) checks details of work and materials and, if necessary, authorizes materials requisition.	
4.			Supervisor enters worker's name(s) on job sheet and records basic details in log book (Job no., address, brief description, time issued and worker's initials).	
5.	C	W_1	Work carried out. Jobbing sheet is returned to supervisor for checking and passed back to receptionist (or other office staff) for cost coding. (Supervisor (DSO) also signs worker's timesheet based on hours worked.)	W_1 weakness: the tenant is not asked to sign that the work has been undertaken and completed to his/her satisfaction. No post-inspection on about 50% of work.
6.	C		Receptionist matches against bottom copy and checks that arithmetic is correct (rate, materials, hours, etc.) and passes to manager or deputy manager for authorization.	
7.		W_2	Authorization is done by signature on the job sheets of the existing HALOs in a pretyped 'passed-for-payment' box or by stamping 'passed-for-payment' on the jobbing sheets originally issued to and still used by the new HALO (W2).	W_2: There is a general lack of custody control over the stamp.
8.			The manager (or deputy) places the authorized job sheets in the internal paid tray for forwarding to the finance section.	
9.	C		Finance clerks file the order and match it against invoice when received. If the two agree payment is initiated.	

Document flow

Tenant — Housing area local office — Building works DSO/local firms (Supervisors)

Prepared — Revised

All the false job sheets were stamped and the top copy sent to the finance section a few days prior to the firm issuing an invoice. In the unlikely event of a query from finance the first point of contact would be the receptionist. In fact, finance section held the new HALO in high regard because, unlike other HALOs nearly all their works invoices could be easily matched to jobbing sheets; the amounts, dates and details always tied up (they were all made up by the receptionist) and they could be paid quickly and simply. Whenever documents from the old HALOs were missing or unstamped, finance section would quote the new HALO as a model of best practice.

Once internal auditors had noticed the lack of control over the stamp and given the relatively high level of jobbing repairs and the known suspicions of the housing directors, they decided to check the diary of visits kept by inspectors against the addresses on the jobbing sheets. This revealed the extent of fraud almost immediately.

The simple but very important control lacking in this case was prenumbered 'orders'. Although the job sheet acted as an order it was probably not thought of in the same light as routine orders for stationery, cement, timber, etc. which in all probability were numbered. Had the job sheets been prenumbered then the inspectors would have noticed that they never saw half of them. Even if the sheets had not been prenumbered but had been given sequential job numbers as work became available this control would have prevented any significant level of false jobbing works.

The 'passed for payment' stamp should, of course, have been kept under the strict control of the person(s) authorized to use it. In this case the manager and probably deputy manager should have kept safe custody of the stamp and not allowed it to be accessed by other junior officers. But stamps like this one often have to be passed to subordinates during sickness, leave, emergencies, etc. and easily become common property.

Closer scrutiny of budgets could also have played a more important part in preventing or detecting this fraud. One is left to wonder whether similar frauds were in place at any other HALO in the authority to which the new HALO belonged before it came under the jurisidiction of Harmborough. Occasional comparisons to similar-sized operations at other locations might well have revealed the apparently poor value for many of the jobbing repairs undertaken at the new HALO. This, indirectly, was what happened on re-organization into Harmborough.

Custody of official stamps, prenumbering of official documents – these are all very routine controls that often get overlooked. They can, depending upon the circumstances, be quite crucial in preventing fraud.

Concluding points

Whatever common elements are identified among the revenue expenditure systems of organizations the scope for variety and for peculiar arrangements seems limitless. This means that no one can anticipate all the risks. In most large organizations the revenue expenditure systems span the responsibilities of several managers. Each manager, it seems, tends to assume that the others are carrying out more checks and controls than is usually the case, or at least the case when a fraud is discovered. Exceptions to normal best practice tend to be tolerated more than would be the case in other well-controlled systems.

Revenue expenditure presents more temptation than most systems. The three most effective methods of deterring frauds in revenue expenditure systems are sound internal controls, regular audit and routine management checks.

7

Revenue income

Introduction

Income is a particularly wide topic in which the scope for fraud and corruption is virtually unlimited. Because of their great variety income frauds tend to be treated in isolation by auditors and managers. In fact the lack of certain key controls is often a common factor in these frauds.

This chapter will be concerned largely with discussing these key controls and the basic risks involved in each of the main types of revenue.

There is an important difference between central government departments and other public bodies. The former, including agencies, are financed largely by 'grant in aid' voted by Parliament.

Tax revenues collected by the Inland Revenue, Customs and Excise and from other sources such as Vehicle Excise Duty are paid into the centralized Consolidated Fund managed by the Bank of England along with borrowings held by the National Loan Fund. These revenues are 'granted' to departments as the various spending programmes progress. Public bodies other than central government departments, are often funded only partly by grants (such as grants paid over from the Department of the Environment to local authorities) and partly by local taxation, fees and charges. For these other bodies sources of revenue are generally far more diverse than for central government departments.

As far as grant transfer between public bodies is concerned there exists a vast and complex system; what an accountant might conceive of as a national bookkeeping exercise. Little in the way of cash or negotiable instruments actually changes hands and the scope for conventional 'income' fraud within this bookkeeping system is limited. However, once outside parties are introduced into the system, at the end-point of, say, rent collection, or distribution of a relocation subsidy, the normal risks discussed in other chapters also apply. Thus for most bodies, 'non-transfer' sources of income present the greatest risk by far. The main scope for fraud and corruption, as with all income systems, occurs at the point of collection, i.e. by initial evasion of payment.

National and local taxation

These areas will be dealt with quite briefly which, given the volume of money involved, may seem a little surprising. The main issue is one of tax evasion including corporation tax, income tax, the council tax, customs duty, value added tax, vehicle excise duty, fuel duty, etc. Except for the few cases that may involve collusion with civil servants this aspect of fraud and corruption falls within the private rather than the public sector and thus outside the scope of this book. This is not to say that civil servants and local government officers never evade tax, rather that being almost whole salaried or waged employees, taxed via PAYE, their scope for evasion is immaterial compared to the wider and more diverse private sector.

Collection records can of course be falsified, but short of bribery on a massive scale, it is difficult to see the motive for any serious level of falsification. The main counter-measures against tax evasion involve completeness of data regarding the tax base and the ability of the collectors or inspectors to verify the details of statements and declarations. Take vehicle excise duty (VED) for example. On first consideration enforcement would seem fairly straightforward. The licensing agency (the DVLA at Swansea) keeps records of all vehicles, their 'keepers' and all drivers – a complete population. All details can actually be checked against the vehicle or, if required, against the driver for such things as age or medical conditions. In practice though even an apparently straightforward example such as VED can have many complications. Registered but unlicensed vehicles may be exempt from VED by being kept off the road and out of use. Numerous weight scales and axle combinations may be misdeclared by heavy goods vehicle operators which, unless the vehicle is subject to a spot check, are likely to go unnoticed on the road. Licences, which usually contain only small typed or handwritten vehicle registration numbers, can easily be transferred between vehicles. Provided that vehicles are not left parked on a public highway for any length of time few passers–by (traffic wardens excepted) are likely to read the printed detail of the licence disc. Perhaps the most costly form of VED evasion is the casual evader who does not bother to relicence for a few months and then claims the vehicle was off the road. Such relatively simple evasion can cost tens of millions of pounds each year.

Tax evasion of local authority taxes (business rates and council tax) suffers from similar verification problems. Often a local tax requires a positive notification or declaration by the taxpayer. This is particularly true where a change of personal circumstances or use of premises occurs. If tax records cannot automatically be cross-checked to other data sources, and often for technical or legal reasons they cannot, then a tax debt may remain completely unrecorded. Here again completeness of the database or of the known population is the main problem. Enforcement agencies will carry out sample checks or circulate all known taxpayers which may well reveal unnotified changes but is much less likely to reveal a completely new tax debtor. Regular 'home' visits are in most cases rather costly compared to the extra tax likely to accrue from discovering the occasional unrecorded lodger, for example.

Corporation tax evasion, or attempted evasion, by commercial bodies within the private sector, from small firms to multinational corporations is on a vastly greater scale than what has been briefly touched upon so far.

Sales, fees and charges

Traditionally these are the areas most prone to public sector fraud among the income gathering functions or public bodies. The level of fees and charges will be set in most cases by statute or by resolution passed by the elected or appointed members of the public body. Occasionally discounts or special offers are available but, largely due to the need to be seen to be fair and electorally accountable, many common private sector marketing practices are not considered acceptable. However trading and profit and loss accounts and commercial-style management are in general becoming more frequently used. Often, this is on the basis of what might be called a 'stand-alone' or self-accounting unit. Direct service organizations, NHS trusts, and government trading funds are examples.

The basic consideration remains the same whatever the style of accounts produced and the risk of fraud and corruption is generally unaffected. However, certain detailed accounting issues are considered later in Chapter 9. Typical revenue income systems might be illustrated as in Figure 7.1.

Each of the three divisions of Figure 7.1 has its own serious risks and (hopefully) key controls to guard against these risks. Generally, separations of duty are difficult to ensure, except perhaps in very large organizations.

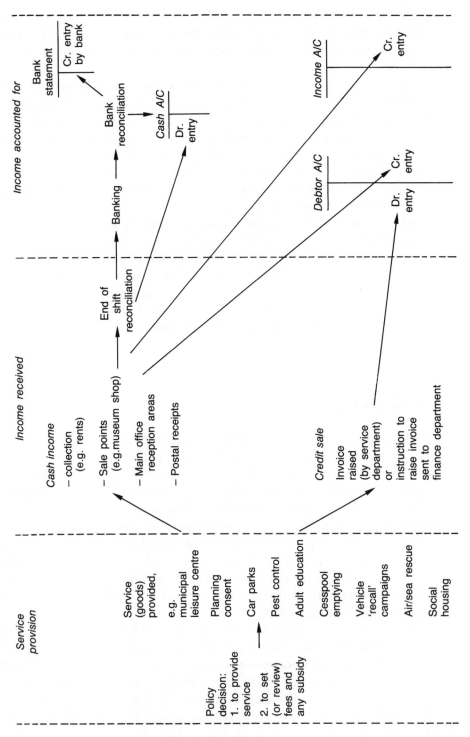

Figure 7.1

Ideally separation should however be encouraged between service provision, income receipt and income accounting.

If, as often arises on small sites, a service is provided and cash or cheques are received directly by the person providing the service, risk of misappropriation is increased.

Officers often hand out tickets for cash, leaflet sales or petty fines for example. Pest control officers and others may accept cash on site. In theory a prenumbered receipt or till roll should always be given when the cash is received. The customer can check the amount receipted agrees with what he or she handed over and the record of receipts issued can be agreed to takings. In practice few people are overly concerned about receipts which may be little more than a till roll. The services provided are not often ones for which the customer may demand a refund, unlike counter sales in most shops. Most fees and charges are levied for services rather than goods, such as the hire of meeting halls, sports facilities, etc. Compared with goods, inadequate services, unless they are persistently so, are far less likely to generate irate customers, who have kept their receipt, demanding back their monies.

Grants and donations

The major grants from central to local government present in general a very low risk of fraudulent abuse. Most are calculated according to formulae based upon the socio-economic characteristics of the local government area and its expenditure on various programmes such as housing or means-tested benefits. Errors can and do occur and some would say this area is particularly prone to errors, but the officers of the body giving or receiving the grant are unlikely to be able to syphon off any significant amounts. Again, as we discussed above, this source of income is but a part of the wider intergovernmental and agency bookkeeping. (Once grants are awarded to private sector and voluntary bodies the risk of fraud increases as is discussed in Chapter Eight). Donations, particularly for disaster and similar *ad hoc* funds are more capable of fraudulent misappropriation, and control over donations should be of a similar standard to income control in general. This is discussed below.

Key control aspects of income

An adequate level of internal control for revenue income systems could be expected to involve most of the following key areas of control 1 to 10, covering

policy, accounting for provision, completeness of income received, accounting for income received and the role of senior management.

Policy

1. The fees and charges (including any nil charges) for all types of goods and services should be subject to periodic, usually at least annual, review. Statutory services or others that are funded by grant from another body – usually a central government department – should also be included in such reviews, as should fully subsidized services provided by the reviewing body.

    Such reviews may form part of a wider budgeting process such as a cyclical 'zero based' or regular activity based budget review. The important control point is that all actual sources of income and all potential sources of income are considered by an appropriate policy-making body, independent of the income-gathering and accounting processes. Local government is a good example. One community may tolerate direct charges for public car parks, galleries, meals-on-wheels, etc. while its neighbour would fund these by full subsidy.

    Regular political accountability acts to reduce the risk of unintentional charges or subsidies; unintentional that is in the sense of not having arisen from positive policy decisions.

    Political accountability also reduces the risks of such unintentional charges as might arise being improperly used or not fully brought to account. This might occur if some form of overcharging is made possible by deliberately or unintentionally allowing incomplete charging policies with an unbudgeted excess of income being used in an unauthorized manner; for example, an unapproved consultation fee that was used to finance bonus payments.

Accounting for provision

2. Review by policy-making bodies should be only the top level of a detailed budgetary review process by officers (usually accountants) not involved in day-to-day income generation or collections. Such a review should encompass:
    (a) the need and viability of charging for each service/product;
    (b) the amount and build-up of the charge or of any subsidy;
    (c) the amount of income or subsidy compared to the original budgeted estimates and any revised estimates.

It is important to note that the key control is in the separation between officers involved in income generation and collection such as property lettings officers, rent collectors and cashiers on the one hand and on the other hand officers involved in the review procedures (a) to (c) mentioned above.

Completeness of income received

A fourth and more detailed review of the trends of income from each source of collection is often undertaken: sometimes by an accountant, sometimes by a budgetary control officer, occasionally by an internal auditor as part of an analytical review. The objective is to identify and investigate unexpected troughs and peaks in sources of regular collection; for example, from direct sales of surplus military equipment or even from such mundane sources as car parks, seaside kiosks, etc. Both unexpected peaks and unexpected troughs may indicate problems. Simple graphs of income over time may reveal sudden changes with no obvious explanation. These should be the subject of discreet but probing enquiry. Should income have been higher in the past? Have staff changed or are better management practices now in place? Is a sudden drop due simply to bad weather, closure for repairs or some less innocent reason?

3. Also usually classified under analytical review are various stock and raw materials usage comparisons. These are generally more applicable to goods than to services. The basic approach involves identifying the mark-up or the relationships between the input cost and the income received. A simple example might be the sale of tennis balls at a leisure centre, as in Table 7.1

Table 7.1 Main stock record – tennis balls

		Initial	In	Out	Bal
Opening Stock b.f.	1.1.X1	A B			200
Issues to cash desk	2 boxes 3.1.X1	D L		24	176
Issues to cash desk	1 box 21.3.X1	D L		12	164
Issues to cash desk	1 box 7.8.X1	D L		12	152
Issues to cash desk	3 boxes 9.10.X1	D L		36	116
Issues to cash desk	4 boxes 17.11.X1	D L		48	68
Issues to cash desk	3 boxes 12.12.X1	C C		36	32
Purchased stock	10 boxes 20.12.X1	A B	120		152
Issues to cash desk	2 boxes 2.1.X2	C C		24	128

In this example AB is the centre's storeman who is responsible for the stock and keeps a card for all stock items. CC and DL are the cashiers, or other staff, who sell the balls.

If income is monitored over the period then, assuming the balls are a standard price, cash banked to the relevant income code can be agreed to stock figures and any peaks and troughs can be queried. In this example, at say £1.00 each, £24.00 (less any returns and stock in hand at point of sale) should have been credited to the relevant income code between 3.1.X1 and 21.3.Xl. Peak sales occurred in late autumn and early winter and a marked trough occurred in the summer.

More sophisticated comparison may be required for most goods and services. Rarely is income credited to a single code or on the basis of a single price per unit. Halls may be rented at prices that vary according to the nature of the functions, the size of the party and at subsidized rates for, say, old age pensioners or charitable organizations. Average mark-ups may prove sufficiently accurate where goods or services are of a similar nature and the price range is relatively small. Reliable relationships can exist (even though exact checks of income owed cannot be made without detailed examination of prime documentation) where the auditor can be confident that error or fraud has not occurred on any material scale. Such a blanket approach to analytical review is often applied to changes in key parameters such as salary percentage increases, business rate poundages, increases in mortgage rates and the like.

The main fraud-related problem that controls of 1 to 3 attempt to offset, i.e. the risk that income will not be fully brought to account, often calls for even more direct internal control than the receiving and budget monitoring procedures discussed so far.

Services may be provided 'on the side' or charges may be levied when the service should be free – from relatively innocent tips to massive backhanders.

4. A fraud at the stage of initial fee collections or levy is likely to be relatively straightforward in concept, such as not putting cash collected through the till or on to a rent card but, to make it worth the fraudster's efforts, such fraud must be perpetrated on a significant scale. So-called 'teeming and lading' whereby one day's (or other period's) receipts are used to cover up shortages in the previous day's takings can be perpetrated for a considerable time (see the Department of Trade's report on the infamous case of the Gray's Building Society) unless regular management or audit surprise checks of cash tills and bankings are undertaken.

5. The only effective way for the fraudster to enable significant fraud to continue is for the initial income received or owed never to be recorded.

Once entries are made on till rolls, debtors ledgers or wherever the likelihood of detection is greatly increased. For this reason one of the most important controls at the initial stages of any income system is for the customer to expect and be issued with prenumbered sequential receipts for goods and services. Receipts should be in at least two parts or copies. The top copy should he handed or posted to the customer. The under (or stub) copy should always be retained and can be checked by management via till rolls, or against income codes, etc. Any missing copies will be immediately apparent.

6. Credit sales are a little more complex in general than cash sales but the same principles apply. The fee-payer should not go unrecorded at the point of agreement, i.e. as soon as a debt arises. An invoice (or instruction to raise an invoice) should be made up or automatically printed out, particularly if the transaction has been generated over the telephone. Like receipts, invoices should be serially numbered and any missing ones should be fully explained. The invoice may itself act as a receipt when payment is eventually forthcoming by ensuring it is annotated with the payment details. In some situations it is not thought worth the effort to physically mark 'paid' on copies of invoices issued once these have been paid (unlike invoices received) or even to show any trail of responsibility indicating the officer who actually agreed that the debt had been paid off. In most enquiries the existence of a computer printout or screen display showing the date of payment and possibly details such as an account number and debtor reference is sufficient to resolve any problems. But in any potential fraud enquiry resulting from income apparently being received (i.e. a credit against the debtor account) but not actually being paid into the cash account, it can be crucial to identify the person responsible for entering the credit (or telling a junior clerk to go ahead and credit the debtor account).

As with authorizing an incoming invoice for creditor accounts payable (see Chapter 6) it is important to have signed authorization (or adequate password controlled screen display) of all credits to outgoing invoices or debtor accounts.

Accounting for income received

The importance of the trail of responsibility mentioned above applies equally as income is processed through each stage in the system.

7. All cash (including cheques, postal orders, etc.) should be accompanied by a detailed breakdown and be signed for on transfer. Ideally the transferor

and transferee should count the cash and sign to say they agree the totals as broken down. If the cash is transferred in a sealed container this too should be signed for by the recipient. Thus if cash is transferred from a receptionist-cashier to a supervising officer for the day's takings to be banked then the till summary, usually an automatic printout, should be agreed to the takings (less any cash float) by the receptionist-cashier and the supervisor, both of whom should sign. In any large cash office this will usually mean staggered shifts so that cashing up and banking can be completed in reasonable time.

8. A separation between the cashier, cash collectors and the officers preparing bankings should be maintained. Otherwise the officer preparing the bankings may be tempted to offset any of his or her cash shortages with another cashier's takings. The only reasonable exception to this rule occurs when officers have to bank directly, often in night safes, perhaps at outstations where the costs of enforcing centralized bankings would be prohibitive. A similar need may arise when officers collect cash for work done on site and cannot guarantee to be back at base before cashing up time. Night safe bankings necessitate reliance upon the integrity and controls of the bank. The author has encountered occasions when such reliance has been called into question.

9. Regular reconciliations should be undertaken between
   (a) cash income recorded as banked;
   (b) the bank account;
   (c) income accounts.
   Regular bank reconciliations, daily, weekly or monthly, will be undertaken in almost any organization and these should quickly reveal any failed or disputed bankings. Reconciliations of takings to the income account is not always undertaken but can be useful in preventing fraud. Reconciliation of (a) to (b) involves conventional cash account to bank account reconciliation undertaken weekly or daily in some organizations. (b) to (c) or (a) to (c) usually takes place less frequently. Sometimes this is made difficult because income is credited to the same account from cash and non-cash sources. Often income levels are monitored for each income code heading but against budgeted income rather than in total against cash actually received. This means that if cash is credited to the wrong accounting code (and then used for unauthorized purposes or to cover up fraudulent misappropriation) this will only be noticed if the accountant monitoring the budgets sees a significant and unexpected overpayment on one code and/or underpayment on another. If a debtor account has previously been raised, good debt collection procedures may reveal the fraud when the payee is chased up for debts he or she has already paid off. It is conceivable that neither of these events would occur (for some time at

least) to reveal the miscoding of income. At various points throughout the cash-handing process it may be possible to misappropriate cash proceeds provided, as is often the case in direct fees income, no debtor account is set up. So long as the misappropriation is covered by diverting other (or excess) funds, again where no debtor account is set up, so that no serious drop in expected income is apparent to the budget monitoring accountants, a fraud may remain unnoticed for a considerable time. Eventually total cash and non-cash income should be reconciled to total income credited to the various income account codes allowing for cash in transit, accruals and timing differences with the bank, by which time it may be very difficult to substantiate who actually took the money. In most public bodies this task is further complicated by numerous year-end journal transfers between different expenditure and income accounts. Such accounts are often identified down to a very detailed 'source code' level to satisfy the demands of political members whose debates often lead to adjustments of the financial budgets. From the foregoing, three basic controls stand out as important (though certainly not foolproof) once cash, including cheques and other value documents have been received:

(a) the issue of prenumbered official receipts in duplicate;
(b) the signed (or otherwise evidenced) agreement of officers involved in transferring cash until it is banked;
(c) frequent reconciliations between monies received, banked, credited to income accounts.

The role of senior management

10. The involvement of senior management directly in controlling income varies greatly. Mostly direct involvement is limited to junior and middle managers. Yet a useful basic control, both before and after cash receipt, is a planned programme of senior management checks, as in the following two examples.

(a) Site visits during anticipated peaks and troughs in demand: do the figures for income appear consistent with conditions of demand encountered in the field? If undertaken unannounced this is one of the few control procedures that can give any degree of assurance that income is not being intercepted prior to recording.

(b) Detailed testing of transactions from samples or selections chosen on a random or judgmental basis. When all is said and done the top managers may ultimately be held accountable for any fraud especially in the eyes of their political masters. They should at least be aware of the main signatories who authorize and control income and the documentation involved. Are any hand-written invoices clearly made out? Are listings made of cheques paid into the bank? These are questions that in the event of a fraud might be asked by politicians, the public/press and, of course, the police.

Sometimes such checking by senior managers may be thought to have little if any value. 'The boss is just nosing about' will be a typical reaction. A deterrent effect may ensue in some, usually poorly run, organizations. If, however, planned management checking is carried out with tact it can have a motivating effect, as very senior managers are seen to have an interest in procedures at a relatively low level. In any event such a programme of checking should be reasonably discreet and, unless very poor practices are encountered, it should not need to be frequent. The dividends from such senior management checks come when things go wrong, as they will occasionally even in the best-run organization, particularly when fraud is known or suspected. In such serious circumstances senior managers who know, at least in outline, of the day-to-day procedures and checks put in place by their subordinate (though often still managerial) colleagues are at a distinct advantage. They should already be able to view events from a wider perspective than the officers involved and so bring breadth and comparative knowledge to bear on the detail that they must then consider. Their learning curve, given their existing knowledge, should be very short, and their authority all the more credible. It must be stressed that this advantage can only be gained by checking and verifying evidence of events not simply by meeting people and listening to their problems necessary though this may be. The senior manager who actually examines, say, maternity leave records and work rosters (for the cash desk, the central accounts department, the licence issuing office or wherever) may see for him or herself that long-term maternity absences are causing a break-down in, say, separation of duties: or alternatively that this definitely is not a problem. Otherwise these visits will probably do no more than confirm that babies are being born and junior and middle managers are finding it difficult (or not as the case may be) to allow their people maternity leave.

Case studies

The first case study of Oldtown Heritage Centre discusses a situation of 'over the counter' fraud. This fraud is generally thought to be more common in the private (usually small retail) sector, but as more commercial sources of income are sought it may well increase in the public sector. The second case considers debtors arising from refunds due to overpayment, a situation fairly common in the public sector.

Case study 7.1 Oldtown Heritage Centre

Oldtown Heritage Centre was originally the Oldtown Museum which also housed a collection of paintings of local artists, some of considerable repute. Oldtown itself was becoming increasingly popular among tourists and as a venue for the arts. Local councillors decided to have under one roof a subsidized museum, gallery, municipal theatre and tourist information centre – The Heritage Centre. This, it was anticipated, would cut the costs of running these as separate establishments. The centre would attract more visitors and trade to each function and to the town in general and provide an opportunity to offer refreshments, souvenirs, etc. at charges that would minimize the need for subsidy. The Heritage Centre contained gift counters which, among the postcards, bottles of Oldtown spring water and trinkets, sold copies of the official Oldtown guide at 50p each. This was a simple but attractive little publication with a centre-spread double page map of Oldtown, a guide to forthcoming theatrical events and the exhibits in the museum/gallery. Most of the costs of production were covered by a few discreet and tasteful advertisements for local hotels, restaurants and the like and the council hoped to make a small contribution from each copy. Unfortunately, the assistant manager, whose office contained a colour photocopier, had similar aspirations.

The colour copier had originally been very useful when notices, posters and programmes advertising public events at the centre and elsewhere in the local authority area ran out. Indeed its legitimate use in this respect, particularly for extra copies of the official Oldtown guide had, no doubt, put the idea of fraudulent use into the assistant manager's mind. The main obstacle to his intentions had been a rigid separation of duties between the cashiers at the two tills in the centre and himself. He or the manager made up the bank paying-in slips and the monies had to be reconciled to the end of shift printouts produced and signed by each cashier. He or the manager would countersign the printouts and sign the paying slips.

The assistant manager, had at first, considered collusion with one or both of the cashiers. In fact this was not necessary. As the months passed after the Heritage Centre had been opened it became increasingly apparent that lunchtime cover would be needed at the tills. From midday until two in the afternoon only one cashier was on duty while one took an hour's lunch break. Rather than recruit a part-time cashier, the assistant manager started covering at the tills. The manager, who was an excellent organizer of events and people, had very little experience of finance. The assistant manager explained that the cost of hiring extra cover would be out of all proportion to the extra revenue and this would probably be criticized by the auditor (which may well have been true). He substituted photocopies for some of the original stock and pocketed any money taken for copied items at his till. Few if any customers bothered to ask for a till receipt. Even when they did and he needed to enter the sale of items on the till the fact that he reconciled his own printout to the bankings meant that no one else was likely to spot that the equal totals were not actually derived from equal castings. Provided he always sold his 'own' stock no stockcheck would indicate takings were unreasonably low for the items sold. The auditors might occasionally have checked till rolls against bankings but he was always careful to ensure 'his' till rolls were difficult to find. He could expect to sell about 100 to 150 guides a week during his shifts, particularly as he tended to make sure that the stock held by the other cashier was likely to run out about midday. At 50p each this was a clear profit of £50 to £75 per week. He had no material costs as the paper and the copying facilities were under his direct control. A few other copiable items sold for a small fee but his main money spinner was the official Oldtown guide.

The manager's suspicions were aroused when the assistant manager was hospitalized following a car accident. Each week the manager received income summaries from the accounts branch at head office showing income against each main product or service. The income against guides and maps rose substantially during the six weeks his assistant was on sick leave. Looking back over earlier records he noticed smaller and shorter peaks during the weeks the assistant manager was on annual leave.

This aroused his curiosity, though his initial reaction was to assume that his assistant manager's absences had coincided with major events. His diary soon refuted this theory. Perhaps his assistant manager was forgetting to stock up on the guide? So, on his return, the manager asked him how sales and stock were.

'Always a poor line – lots of stock left over,' was the reply. 'Except when you're not here,' thought the manager, his suspicions now aroused. The manager called in the internal auditor. Together they checked the detail of the tally rolls from the tills against the reconciliations of the assistant manager and found some discrepancies relating to times when till slips had been requested, or possibly when other staff had been close by the assistant manager when he was serving a customer and would have noticed if he had not issued a receipt. They counted the stock of guides on several occasions prior to the lunch break shift of the assistant manager and the manager made rough estimates of the number of customers who appeared to be purchasing them, about twenty or so each time. The auditor asked the assistant manager how sales of various items including guides, were going. The guides, he was told by the assistant manager, averaged about one or two per hour. Together the auditor and manager searched the assistant manager's office while he was still on till duty and found a cupboard full of guides, all reasonably good colour photocopies but on close examination obviously not produced by the printers. The staples were out of alignment and the edges contained a narrow black rim where the originals did not quite correspond to the size of the standard A4 paper used.

The assistant manager was disciplined and dismissed.

The main weakness that led to this case was the lack of separation of duties over cash accounting. The manager, or even perhaps one of the cashiers, should have counted the takings (entering the totals on the bank paying-in slip) and checked these to the printout and the summary, e.g.

Tally roll total + float = total cash in till = bankings plus float.

All three totals should have been entered on the reconciliation sheets with checkable explanations of any adjustments.

Even if this had been done the assistant manager might actually have been able to pocket cash before his shift ended, though with another cashier present at cashing up this would have been difficult to achieve on a large scale.

For discrete items coded to a separate income code auditors often check stock movement against income. Basically the sum of opening stock (number) plus additional item purchases less the closing stock multiplied by the selling price should equal income. In this case this method would have been ineffective as the assistant manager supplied his own stocks.

Case study 7.2 The creche grant scheme

There are a great many government grants and rebates available, administered by various departments of state, for a wide variety of purposes. Occasionally these are *ad hoc* but most are of a recurring nature. They range from fuel duty rebates for bus operators in rural areas to grants to other public bodies for urban renewal. The arrangements, although largely a matter of expenditure consideration (see Chapter 6) rather than income, often involve substantiation of the income of the grant-aided body and direct income due to the department from refunds.

The government has decided that employers who are willing to provide a creche for working mothers in their employment will be entitled to a grant of 50% towards any capital costs and all direct revenue costs (mainly the costs of a full-time nursery nurse and rent of suitable premises).

Shortly after the scheme was introduced the national economy went into a relatively sudden and unexpected economic slump. The rate of company bankruptcies increased dramatically, including those among companies operating the creche grant scheme. It had always been anticipated that a small number of companies might start up but not be able to continue a creche and an executive officer (EO) had been designated to chase up any grant monies due to be refunded. The senior executive officer (SEO) responsible for the officer collecting the refunds noticed a serious backlog of work was outstanding after only the first two months of the year. He suggested that a further one or two staff be recruited, hopefully on a temporary basis, to help clear the backlog. To his surprise the EO told him that the backlog was due mainly to his suffering from an influenza virus rather than the economic downturn. He assured the SEO that with some overtime he should be able to reduce the backlog to a month or so at most. The SEO, a little reluctantly, agreed to give the EO a further three months during which time he, the SEO, would keep a close watch on the backlog.

Over the next three months the backlog did indeed appear to be reducing at a substantial rate. Each week the EO presented the SEO with a case-load summary showing fewer and fewer outstanding cases. Most firms who were no longer able to proceed with the creche scheme appeared willing to refund all, or nearly all, of the grant monies. In many cases there were letters from company officials mentioning cheques enclosed for the relevant amounts. By the end of the three months the SEO, who had a great many other problems on his mind, was grateful that one more potential headache had abated.

At this point the EO announced – much to the SEO's disappointment – that he had found another job abroad. He offered to work his full notice but explained that his new employers would be grateful if he could start as soon as possible. Arrangements were made to facilitate his departure a week later.

The creche scheme refunds were classified as 'appropriation-in-aid'. This means that they could be treated as income by the government department concerned, rather than having to be surrendered to the government's consolidated fund as so-called 'extra receipts'. A few days after the EO had departed and before his replacement arrived, the SEO received a telephone call from a colleague in the accounts branch asking whether much income has been received from refunds as they were about half way through the financial year. The original estimate mentioned approximately £50 000 may be due. (The colleague had no obvious way of deducing that the rise in companies' financial problems would mean that many more than anticipated would back out of the scheme and therefore be required to make a refund.)

After some searching the SEO could find no record of banking the sums listed as received. In fact the list of receipts itself seemed incomplete and he then recalled that the only detailed records shown to him were breakdowns of case-loads. He hurriedly scanned through the EO's desk instructions and noted that an under-copy receipt should have been filed on each case file. After fumbling further through the contents of the former EO's desk he found the key to a large filing cabinet containing the case files, about 600 in all. He undid the lock, the double doors of the cabinet sprang apart and the SEO was swamped with files – all of which contained duly signed and authorized copy receipts.

His initial relief soon dissipated when he compared the amounts receipted to the amounts granted according to the earlier documents on each file, usually less than half, sometimes much less. Worse still each receipt has been made out 'in full and final settlement of any claim'.

The internal audit section with the help of the SEO pieced together the following scenario and promptly called in the police.

The EO after starting off quite honestly begins to 'go bent', perhaps after receiving bribes from desperate businessmen trying to avoid bankruptcy. He knows that accounts branch are not expecting any substantial monies to be paid over 'in the books', at least for a few more months. Occasionally he accepts and pays over to accounts branch receipts for those companies who have paid the whole amount on a genuine basis.

Most companies are eager to accept a generously lower settlement than the total grant due to be refunded especially if the revenue element is quite large. They did not (or did not want to) question the EO's authority – he was a genuine officer and the receipt was an official and binding one. Many firms were happy to pay cash.

The EO had, quite properly, opened a bank account in the name of his employers. He was required to make visits to attempt recovery of the monies and this account was intended to cover his expenses. The bank had a letter from the SEO authorizing the account to be operated by the EO. But this letter mentioned a credit ceiling and required monthly statements to be sent to the accounts office. The EO had simply photocopied a similar letter with the SEO's signature; altered the banking details and the details of the accounts office to his own office; recopied the altered letter so that no erasing marks were evident and inked over the signature so that it appeared to be an original. He used this forgery to open another account into which he paid, and withdrew any cheques.

The main factors facilitating this fraud were (not necessarily in order of importance) the following.

1. No one had budgeted for large sums to be recovered and the accountants monitoring the income were not expecting substantial (if any) sums.
2. The EO was left largely unsupervised despite the fact that the SEO expected him to be overworked.
3. In particular, no separation of duties existed between the assessment of amounts due and the collection and receipting of monies paid.

During the time the EO was employed on this work (just over six months) no senior officer, or indeed any peer, reviewed the detailed files or questioned the actual takings.

Eventually the EO would probably have been found out: the bank's own auditors may have circularized the department to confirm year-end balances; the EO may have been taken sick; the SEO would, eventually, have taken a closer interest in the EO's work; and the department's own auditors would have asked to see the files.

In the meantime the EO made off with various proportions of salary, rental, capital, etc. – costs granted to and now refunded by the 600 or so firms. Say 600 firms at an average £5000 – this totals £3 000 000!

Concluding points

For ordinary revenue income the most difficult problem, from the viewpoint of preventing fraud and corruption, is ensuring completeness. The organization may not be aware of all the income due and two key controls are recurrent in helping to prevent this – supervision of activities (including management checks) and separation of duties. In particular no single officer should control debt-generating activities, invoicing and cash receipting.

In the private sector matters affecting income and cash flow into the organization affect its lifeblood and are generally at the very top of senior management priorities. In the public sector macro-level considerations of income, especially taxation levels, are important but the cash flow aspects are generally secondary matters compared with issues surrounding expenditure. Political debates often revolve around spending plans, less so cash flow projections. Senior managers are frequently involved in implementing changes in expenditure programmes geared to the latest policy objectives. Objectives change continuously without the constancy of market-driven long-term objectives such as profit maximization or market share maximization. Such shifting sands may be inevitable in a free political system but the special risks at the micro-level should not be forgotten.

8

Means-tested benefits and grants

Introduction

A wide range of grants, benefits, allowances, subsidy payments, etc. are made to individuals, families and organizations including student grants, housing benefits, new business grants, grants to parish councils and aid to foreign countries. Most of these are subject to some form of means testing whether in fine detail or in more general terms and conditions.

This is a particularly difficult area in relation to fraud and corruption. The root of the problem, like that of tax evasion, (see Chapter 7) lies outside the public sector itself. In this case it is to do with the honesty of individual citizens or organizations acting as claimants.

False claims for grants and benefits, caused either directly or by omitting to notify a public body of a relevant change in circumstances, are almost encouraged by some conditions and are, it is generally accepted, not cost-effective to prevent altogether. In spite of this pessimistic perception it is both possible and cost-effective to put into operation a number of key controls and to channel resources (usually labour) to both detective and preventative work in areas where they are likely to provide good value for money.

Redistribution

The overall purpose of benefits and grants is redistribution of national or local resources. Most governments have adopted policies of redistribution of income or wealth for varying reasons. The funding of popular social and philanthropic causes tends to be expected by voters whether they themselves are beneficiaries, think they may be possible beneficiaries at some future date, or simply consider the causes to be justifiable and worth paying for. Although not all redistributed benefits are means tested the risk of widespread fraud and corruption for, say, the universally provided child benefit are minimal compared to means-tested housing benefits. For the former one has only to prove the existence of a dependent child; for the latter a relatively large number of conditions regarding rents or mortgages paid, tenancy, residence, income, savings, etc. have to be disclosed and verified. It is therefore the aim of this chapter to concentrate wholly on means-tested benefits though much of what is written applies to both types.

The mechanics of redistribution are invariably controlled by the state. This is likely to remain true even if public agencies and private firms were asked to compete for a benefit franchise. Such a situation runs up against the problems of self-interest and the basis of rewarding such an agency or firm, (see Chapter 2) as a conflict of interest is likely to arise. For example, if a standard rate is paid for processing a claim then what would be the incentive to check the validity of the claim in detail? A government inspectorate or similar independent persons such as private management consultants or auditors could be asked to audit and certify the records of the agency; but would the cost of this be outweighed by the benefits of competition? The answer may depend very much on what other work was undertaken by the agency or by the consultants or auditors. In any event, the act of compulsory redistribution, whoever performs it, may be considered the role of the state in a modern society and as such may be divided into the categories displayed in Figure 8.1.

Only a few examples are shown, though in Britain and most other developed countries these are subject to virtually continuous legislative change. Benefits and grants come and go as parties and policies and economic conditions change. A complex and confusing set of terminology and regulations is continually revised, amended, re-interpreted (often by the courts or any one of a number of tribunals) and subject to varying definitions of means. Age is sometimes taken as synonymous with need; some grants such as tree planting grants, are awarded on the basis of benefits to others who remain undefined or to the environment, i.e. the community in general.

Any attempt to consider all the detailed regulatory aspects of benefits and grants on an individual basis would need to be voluminous, to say the least.

Recipient	Examples of benefits and grants
Individual	Income support, community charge benefit, various disablement allowances
Family	Family credit, housing benefit, child benefit
Commercial organizations	City grants, research grants, rural development grants
Political unit	Selective aid programmes to developing countries, grants to voluntary bodies, grants from local government to parishes
Owners or 'custodians' of property	Renovation grants, grants to voluntary bodies

Note: some overlap in definition is inevitable in what is invariably a fluid situation

Figure 8.1

Certainly such detailed consideration is beyond the scope of this work. Fortunately sufficient important procedures and key controls are repeated to make a generalized summary worthwhile.

Summary of organizational controls

All claims relating to a single claimant should be filed together (or clearly cross-referenced). Quite often information supplied by the claimant or verified by a case officer in relation to one claim will, in cases of fraud, contradict or call into question that of another claim. Also, if one claim is found to be fraudulent in a hitherto unsuspected manner it is quite likely that some other similar claims will also be affected. Likely cases may involve housing benefits, income support or community charge benefit, for example. Sometimes, as with income support and housing benefit, these benefits are administered by different public bodies. While close liaison between officers and prompt notifications of changes in circumstances may be possible, the files and data will be kept separately and are, of course, subject to the provisions of the Data Protection Act 1984 (see Chapter 5).

No single officer should be involved in processing and authorizing a complete claim. As with most separation of duties this can be difficult to achieve in situations of very limited resources. However, most benefits are processed by departments with numerous staff dedicated to processing claims on the basis of area, alphabetic order, or a similar broad division. It is usually feasible for the work to be separated into:

1. basic review and initial enquiry;
2. site or home visit;
3. final review and authorization of entitlement letter, exchange of agreement, etc.

It is usually cost-effective for the final authorization and any site visit to be carried out by officers not involved in the initial receipt and vetting of the claim. Often complications arise and costly or disputed items have to be referred to a senior officer for clarification which is a further natural separation feature. Ideally the powers of junior staff and circumstances requiring the attention of senior officers should be clearly documented and explained to new recruits.

As a general management control, where numerous cases are being processed daily (and especially if a separation of duties is difficult to maintain) a random selection of cases should be checked by management. Selection should ensure a range and frequency of cases sufficient to form a reliable opinion on the remainder. It may well be worthwhile in practice to choose a small statistical sample or use a combination of randomly selected statistical samples and a judgmental selection from high risk types.

Claim reference numbers should be issued in sequence as soon as a claim is received. Claims that are, or become, invalid should be retained for the relevant statutory period or audit-required period, whichever is the greater. Any delay in the allocation of a number while the claim is being handled and perhaps given its initial vetting adds to the risk of loss, misfiling and, most importantly from our viewpoint, the risk of suppression or false amendment of the claim itself or any subsequent cancelling or amending of documents received during these initial stages. Sometimes an excuse is made along the lines of 'a number can not be allocated until the claim has been entered on the computer, or after it has been checked'. This usually means that it does not get numbered until everything has been cleared up and it can be processed without a hitch. In most cases this involves a significant time, e.g. more than an hour or so. In the days of batch processing some credence may have been attached to such an excuse; rarely so today. If a claim must be delayed before numbering, it should be given a short-term reference which should usually be incorporated in its final reference number.

Adequate staff/supervisory ratios must be maintained. Like most controls this is simply good management practice. It is not difficult to see that in an environment where rules are changing, revised rates are being introduced intermittently and often staff turnover rates are fairly high, the work needs to be closely supervised. Most means-tested benefits are such that false case files or unamended files could produce a lucrative temptation for what are, almost inevitably, fairly low paid clerks. Case study 3.2 provided an example of this type of fraud based on false payroll files.

Case papers

Criticism is sometimes levelled at the poor standard of working papers associated with grants and means-tested benefits. Exceptions can and do occur. But, given their importance to the claimant and the risk of subsequent court or tribunal proceedings, it is surprising if due care and attention is not paid to the quality of case papers. Pressure to attain a quick turn-around of case-load, or low staff morale, or the fact that the officer first dealing with the case is unlikely to deal personally with any appeal or court action, may be among the causes. Whatever the cause, untidy and disorganized case papers provide ready camouflage for fraud. Errors and uncertainty will become acceptable, first upon a small scale, later becoming more widespread. Fraud perpetrated externally by the claimant will become less easily spotted. Confirmations of income, rents, acreage, damage, dependants or whatever will become delayed, then missing until after the case has been decided, and then in some cases it may not be sought at all. The author has come across situations where 'error correction teams' or 'control sections' have been set up within the benefit or grants administering bodies. This step may at first have some deterrent effect, though in practice it is more likely to be a negative influence and lead to dependence upon the error correction team to act as a safety net, so encouraging even more lax attitudes to the quality of work. In most normal circumstances errors should be very infrequent or well within the capability of motivated staff and diligent supervision or management to reduce to acceptable levels. Quite the opposite effect to that of error correction teams can be obtained if the emphasis is placed upon quality control or quality enhancement. This may be achieved by existing officers or may in some organizations be best achieved by seconding officers from other departments to work for specified periods as part of a separate quality control team. The critical difference, from the viewpoint of both errors and deliberate fraud, is that every set of case papers or at least examples of the work of every officer (including computer-held records) should be assessed from a quality viewpoint whether it contains errors or not. Officers should be made aware of high standards, not merely poor performance. Obviously both management and unions may be able to use such findings to reward or seek rewards for enhanced performance or productivity. Basically, error correction safety nets if they are in place should be replaced as soon as possible by quality motivations designed to reverse any trend to poor quality case papers.

Some of the more important types of working papers are mentioned in the checklist in Appendix 8.1.

Post-award work

Notification

The notification of the final award is usually a crucial stage. This may refer to a single grant payment or to an on-going weekly benefit or some combination of intermittent payments. Ideally, a senior manager, or panel of adjudicators, or some other person(s) outside the receiving and checking of the claim should give the final approval, albeit that this is done on the advice and calculations of the officers involved in processing the claim. The person(s) involved in finally approving the amount and conditions, if any, attached to the award constitute a separation of duties that provides one further safeguard against the improper or irregular claim. Such persons usually develop a feeling for what is acceptable in various circumstances particularly if, as is usually the case, they have themselves been involved in processing similar claims or grants in the past and have over the years come to experience a wide variety of circumstances and processing procedures. As with cheque payments, discussed below, the final notification should not be handed back to the officer involved in processing the claim but should be posted out to the claimant.

Changes in circumstances

The system should have key controls that draw attention to changes in circumstances. These are with a few exceptions more appropriate to on-going benefit than to single payment grant claims. Such controls might involve periodic reassessments of circumstances, such as reassessment of entitlement to housing benefit. Another example might be comparisons between council rent or tax accounts and benefit claims, or even inter-body comparisons involving employers, and the Inland Revenue. Inter-body comparisons would of course need to be carefully considered in the light of the Data Protection Act 1984 and if appropriate the current Official Secrets regulations.

Investigation officers

Most benefit administrating organizations maintain some form of investigatory arm, usually under the control of senior management, though at times internal audit or even external audit may be called upon to advise. It is crucial in preventing fraud and corruption that neither the investigating officers themselves, nor the officers processing the claims, are able to have complete control over which cases are investigated or the level of investigation involved. Senior management should set down strict guidelines on the conduct of investigations and should ultimately determine which cases are allocated to the investigating officer. If it is not practically feasible for managers at an independent level to be involved in determining the choice of each case, strict guidelines should be set down for the selection procedures and the actual selection should be subject to periodic management review. The purpose of such provision is to encourage and maintain impartiality and accountability. Fortunately, in most circumstances, these objectives coincide with good management objectives. A manager may consider it important that all investigation officers get a fair share of difficult cases, or deal with cases most suited to their particular specialist skills, or whatever criteria he or she requires. Provided these are objectively set criteria designed to meet corporate objectives, and the manager issues appropriate instructions and takes steps to ensure these are followed, the risk of partiality and any consequent corruption is likely to be minimized.

Much investigatory work involves pre-award as well as post-award situations. The topic has to be tackled at post-award as most of the investigatory work relating to cases of fraud is undertaken at this stage though, of course, preventative work may well have been undertaken at an early stage.

Cheques

Any direct cheque payments should not be routed back via the officers responsible for processing. This is a standard key control for all payments systems (see Chapter 6).

Any cheques returned because of non-delivery, recipient 'gone away', wrong address, etc. should, as with cheques posted out and for the same reasons, not be routed directly to the officers responsible for processing. All cheques should be crossed 'Not transferable – A/C payee only'.

Follow-up visits

For grants and benefits follow-up visits are often standard practice, as part of the post-assessment of work done or in order to confirm changes in circumstances. Often these visits may act as a deterrent to fraud and generally should be performed by officers not previously involved in the case. Apart from reducing the risk of collusion this separation of duties offers the chance for a second professional opinion and for the beneficiary to voice any concerns to a new face. Except in the most complicated of cases these advantages usually offset any additional costs of familiarization required of a new officer.

Analytical (trend) reviews

Sometimes the wood can be missed for the trees, especially when staff are under pressure from the short-term requirements of individual case-loads and regular management reports. Analytical review considers the broad picture shown by trends over time and comparisons to other related data. This can be as simple or as complicated as the individual manager thinks is merited (or has the time for). From the viewpoint of fraud the comparisons offer a chance to consider why changes in one variable, say, a disability allowance have not brought about the expected changes in a related variable, say, demand for home helps for the disabled. The use of an analytical review tends to be rather limited either as a preventative or a detective aid in combating individual cases of fraud and corruption but it can be effective when considering the likely validity of allegations of widespread malpractice, particularly when one variable measures a means and the other measures the cost of a benefit. For further references on analytical review see the Bibliography, particularly Jones and Bates (1990).

Case study

Only one detailed case study is given and this is given mainly to provoke the reader's thoughts on the variety of topics that this one area can encompass. As explained later the diversity of fraud related to means-tested benefits and grants warrants regular updating from published sources.

Case Study 8.1 Grants for irrigation projects

Under a multilateral aid agreement between the United Kingdom and several African countries severely affected by drought, grants are provided for irrigation schemes. This is done on the basis of a formula that takes into account national per capita income, the proportion of the schemes' cost raised by the recipients of the grant (including other donations) and the cost of purchases (capital and first year revenue) made from companies designated as UK owned for the purposes of this particular agreement. The formula determines the proportion each of the recipient and donor nations contributes towards the estimated total costs of each scheme.

The national per capita incomes of the various recipient countries are taken from published sources and are in any case estimated figures. However, the total estimated project cost, the proportions of this total funded by the UK, other donors or the recipient nation, and the costs of purchases from UK companies can all, in theory, be manipulated to favour the UK, other donors (if any) or the recipient. Approximately £20 million has been allocated to this type of aid.

Each scheme prepares separate 'stage claims' which are sent to the sponsoring government department, as the scheme progresses. The total value of the grant has been worked out on the basis of estimated figures. At the start of the scheme stage claims should contain a certified account that the scheme has been completed to an agreed stage and funding is on target. Variations in cost (usually overruns) are considered by the sponsoring department for additional funding in accordance with the formula. The certification of the stage claims is usually undertaken by the government auditors of the recipient nation.

At first sight these arrangements may seem quite adequate to ensure an optimum distribution of limited resources between the UK, other donors and the recipient, always provided the formula is agreed by all to be fair. The main risk with such inter-governmental arrangements is that while they may be well suited to one nation with the ethos and usually the controlling influence of a single government they may be totally unsuited to another, say the recipient nation. Here are some examples.

1. The external audit of the UK government by the NAO is generally considered to have a high degree of independence. This may not be the case in other countries where audit may simply be seen as checking undertaken by the government into its own financial affairs to ensure they are conducted in its (the government's) best interest. This is quite different from audit by an independent body not under government control.

2. How are costs to be measured? Stock valuations are notoriously difficult as are valuations of work in progress. The problems of cost measurement are difficult enough in the UK; in an international context where each party has differing accounting conventions and financial incentives to interpret terms in its favour these problems are likely to be multiplied. To some extent cost ceilings can be imposed by the donor but if this leads to a partly finished project then all the sums spent so far might have been wasted and it is usually more acceptable politically to make an increased contribution.

3. Irrespective of problems of interpretation of terms such as costs, values, profits, etc. (which to some extent can be catered for by strict wording and agreed arbitration procedures) further problems of information-gathering are likely to arise. Information originally envisaged may be impractical to obtain in the field situation. Foreign companies may not keep the types of records envisaged or may not supply them on time. Records may change in translation, or over time as new companies and managers arrive to take part in, or take over, the projects.

4. Any audit visits on behalf of the donor will of necessity have to be agreed well in advance and unless the auditors are familiar with the language and custom of the host nations they are likely to be of limited value compared to home audits. Permanent representation on the project is likely to be required if any reasonable measure of control or effective monitoring is thought necessary.

All these problems and the myriad of complications implied in any individual case apply when all parties are assumed to be honest. In this case study two major areas of dishonesty arise and will be examined.

The most obvious and frequent area of corruption was the simple siphoning off of funds. The sheer lack of reliable records and the inability of the UK government representatives to value goods and services at the going (i.e. local) rate enabled as much as 60% of some payments to be used to line the pockets of middlemen and others. In fact, it is open to question as to whether or not corruption, in the deliberate and malicious sense of the word, actually occurred.

Officials more familiar with some of the local schemes pointed out that to some of those involved it might seem that the UK authorities interpreted valid cost in term of their own legal systems and peculiar national, even Christian, values. Such an approach merely served to omit some quite normal costs associated with widely accepted behaviour including bribery in the recipient nation.

It is certainly true that a corrupt or fraudulent action in one nation's cultural and perhaps legal environment may be quite acceptable in another. This much leeway in interpretation any multinational organization or international trading company might acknowledge. Aid, however, does not, it might be argued, fall into the same category as just any other international transaction.

The donor might well feel entitled to assume that the conditions of the aid will be interpreted in a manner that meets the donor's rather than the recipient's expectations. The donor is after all acting in a largely voluntary capacity, unlike a multinational company. The donor, it might be argued by those who hold this view, should at the very least be made aware in advance of the donation of the likely unanticipated (on the donor's part) uses to which these funds will be put.

The second major area of corruption concerned the listing of UK firms. A listing which, one is bound to admit, begins to call into question the donor's disinterested altruism in funding the aid. Giving some form of favourable advantage to companies from donor nations is not an unusual convention and the listing of approved UK firms means that while a recipient country could order equipment that they could not themselves supply from any foreign supplier by using a UK supplier, the UK government would be prepared to increase its funding to the relevant scheme. The risk of corruption in this case was caused by an inadequate definition of a UK firm. In practice there was nothing to prevent a non-UK company setting up a UK subsidiary, or using one already in existence, to channel goods and services to the recipient nation; goods that were in effect produced and marketed by non-UK companies. The UK subsidiary company merely acted as a front when applying to sell the goods or services to the managers in charge of the scheme.

Summary of case study

In the first area of corruption, the siphoning off of funds, lack of management control in general and timely and accurate cost data in particular are largely to blame. However, it is difficult to see, certainly once a project is up and running, how such management information can be imposed upon existing arrangements without significant extra costs and possibly serious delays. In practice the feasibility and desirability of obtaining the information required would depend largely upon the scale and duration of the project. The larger (in cost terms) and longer the project the more desirable and feasible it is likely to be to obtain the required information. The second area of corruption, the definition of a UK firm, is much less of an on-going problem than the first. It is basically a matter of closing a loophole, though it is unlikely that any extra funding provided before the loophole is closed can be justifiably reclaimed. Ideally an independent financial assessment from a financial enquiry agency could be obtained. Alternatively the companies bidding successfully for work on a scheme could be contacted directly to provide proof of their controlling interests.

In both areas of corruption the problems encountered by the donor stem from a lack of clear understanding of the culture and attitudes of the recipient and the firms involved, due, possibly, to the lack of experience or precedents in similar situations.

Regular causes of means-tested fraud

Rather than provide the reader with a case study relating to at most one or two types of means-tested benefit the variety of fraud occurring in this area can best be appreciated by considering the numerous cases reported. Examples are published in the 'Fraud' pages of *Public Finance and Accountancy* and Audit Viewpoint, both published by CIPFA, or the Audit Commission's information circulars. A brief synopsis of some of the main causes is given below.

1. Lack of separation of duties in the claim processing departments leading to:
   (a) fictitious cases;
   (b) deliberate overpayments;
   (c) deliberate non-actioning of cancellation orders;
   (d) deliberate failure to notify other agencies.

2. Lack of resources or poorly targeted resources leading to:
   (a) inability to deter or detect claimant dishonesty;
   (b) lack of separation of duties as in 1 above.

3. Routing of outgoing cheques, confirmation letters, enquiry, letters, etc. back through the hands of the officers processing the claim rather than posting out through the normal postal arrangements leading to:
   (a) interception of payment for fictitious or deliberately overpaid cases;
   (b) maintenance of a fictitious case or the deliberate failure to action cancellations orders.

4. Collusion between:
   (a) the claimant and officers (especially where officers deal with the cases of family or friends);
   (b) the claimant and a third party such as an estate agent, solicitor, landlord or employer;
   (c) officer and officer, e.g. processing clerk and investigation officer.

5. Lack of evidence of the operation of internal control particularly of authorizations. Such causes include:
   (a) lack of an adequate audit trail particularly during computer updating;
   (b) failure to obtain first-hand evidence of circumstances from bank accounts, rent books, home visits, etc.

6. Lack of regular liaison between different government agencies leading to:
   (a) incomplete information passed from, say, the Department of Social Security to local authorities;
   (b) incomplete cross-checking of common data such as address, income, needs assessments, etc.
   (c) fraud being detected by one agency but not being notified to another affected body.

Experienced managers and experts will no doubt be able to envisage other causes. The list is virtually endless given the changing regulatory position.

Concluding points

Relatively few frauds in this area are perpetrated entirely within an organization by its own employees. Most involve claimant dishonesty. Very little can be done by an organization to alter the standards of honesty of their clients in this respect, but given that many claimants succumb to dishonesty partly at least because the systems involved are easy to manipulate or are managed and controlled in a lax or inconsistent manner, much can be done to prevent temptation arising and to deter future cases once a fraud is discovered.

In particular a chain of responsibility should involve more than one officer from initial claim assessment to payment (or initiation of a regular stream of payments). This responsibility should be clearly evidenced as should any checks undertaken by investigating officers, management or supervisors. What, after all, is the point of carrying out constructive and often diligent work if nothing of it remains from which to gain recognition or judge the need for change or future efforts?

Appendix 8.1 Checklist – fraud prevention controls for means-tested grants and benefits

Organization

1. Are all claims relating to a single individual or organization filed together?
2. Are all types of claim dealt with by the same group of officers? If not, on what basis do they specialize?
3. Are reference numbers promptly issued in strict sequence to each initial claim?
4. Consider the organization's family tree: do staff-to-supervisor ratios appear adequate?

Case papers

5. Are all claims, including notifications of changes in circumstances, on a standard official form?
6. Are forms prenumbered?
7. Are all forms given the sequential claim number immediately on receipt (see 3)?
8. Are all claims signed and dated by the claimant or by a recognized official on behalf of the claiming body?
9. Are all the relevant documents that are transferred between organizations, including cancellations of entitlement by one body, stamped or signed or otherwise authenticated by an identifiable officer before posting out to another body?
10. Is a log kept or a date stamp used for all incoming claims, showing date received, department, etc.?
11. Is any manually performed benefit calculation clearly laid out?
12. Are the computer input values (e.g. 'applicable amounts' relating to housing renovation grants and housing benefit) clearly set down when the calculation is done by computer?
13. Can the officer performing a calculation or inputting data to a computer be easily identified?
14. Is any computer program adequate in respect of 'data vet' checks (e.g. reasonableness or ceilings for income)?
15. Are any manual calculations checked by a second officer?
16. Are input details checked by a second officer?

17. What evidence (including photocopies) is retained on file for such factors as:
    (a) rents, e.g. rent book or lease?
    (b) capital, e.g. Building Society/Bank Statement?
    (c) income e.g. wage slip?
    (d) status, e.g. student?
    (e) family circumstances (if applicable)?
    (f) ownership of land or property, e.g. deeds?
18. Are copies of all correspondence (outgoing) traceable to the originating officer, e.g. by reference?
19. Are key original and copy documents, e.g. letters confirming awards or letters of agreement, signed?
20. Is a complete list made of all incoming actionable documents, e.g. housing benefit cancellation certificates sent to local authorities from the Department of Social Security?
21. What evidence is filed to show the extent of any supervisor or management checking?
22. Is a diary or list of home visits or site inspections kept? (Visiting officers' notes should indicate the name of the officer, the time and date, and the conclusions reached including supporting document references.)
23. Are such visits (as at 22 above) undertaken by an officer not otherwise involved in the case?
24. Is it possible to confirm that cheques are not returned to the hands of the claim-processing or visiting officers after payment has been initiated?
25. Are all cheques crossed 'A/C payee only not transferable'?
26. Are any cheques intercepted for last minute alteration or cancellation fully recorded and properly authorized?
27. Are any control totals affected by 26 above promptly amended?
28. Are all cheques that have been returned to the funding organization, and the explanation, recorded in an independently kept register?
29. Are all spoilt cheques checked and authorized by an officer not responsible for generating the replacement?
30. Is there any mechanism for ensuring that all suitable cases, e.g. recovery of over-payment cases, are handed to independent investigating officers?

9

The main accounting function

Introduction

The preparation and nature of accounts is not obviously a topic worth a separate chapter in a work of this kind. Accounts may range from financial ones published after the year end to the more frequent, usually monthly, management accounts ('out-turn' statements as they are sometimes quaintly called in government circles). From the point of view of combating fraud and corruption an organization's accounts are really no more than another set of key controls; and yet, they are such prominent controls and are prepared, used (and abused) in so many and diverse ways, that to treat the accounts in the same manner as, say, the separation of duties within an organization would seem to lack any practical justification.

The accounts being, essentially, a financial picture of an organization's efforts and achievements to date cannot cause or prevent fraud and corruption, any more than can a photograph of a government building. The accountant's decisions of what to include in the picture and, sometimes, to whom the picture should be shown are of course quite a different matter. For the time being we shall assume, with some unavoidable rashness, the accountant to be a completely honest and professional figure. As far as possible the reader will be spared the intricacies of accounting arguments on what form the accounts should take and how the figures should be described, measured, presented and used. Rather we will concentrate on the basic mechanics of public sector accounting and drawing attention to typical areas of control that would enable such an honest and professional accountant to make a very significant contribution to preventing fraud and corruption. Anything more would, the author feels, require a separate book to do justice to public sector accounting (see Further reading).

The purpose and objectives of the main accounting function

Right at the start, despite what has been said about keeping to the basic mechanics of public sector accounting, we cannot avoid considering a fundamental question of theory: what purpose do the accounts serve? Even the mechanics must have a purpose which must be appreciated, at least at a basic level, if the mechanics themselves are to be understood. The purpose of an organization's published accounts is undoubtedly one of public accountability – to inform the reader of its financial affairs. Beyond this most general of statements the purpose becomes somewhat hazy and often hotly debated, not least when a major fraud is uncovered. Questions arise such as to whom should the accounts be directed? What information should they portray? To what level of detail? On what basis should this or that particular figure be calculated? There are probably as many answers to questions such as these as there are accountants. Professional bodies give guidance that should be followed especially in respect of what figures should be included and the basis of their calculation. But even this leaves much to be interpreted and debated.

For convenience let us say that acceptable answers can be found to the above. This still leaves the more practical question to be answered (on which hopefully agreement is easier to reach): what are the objectives of the main accounting system? Let us first consider what is meant by main accounting system. This usually refers to the final arrangements for collating and accumulating the figures produced by other feeder systems into the annual published accounts and estimates and any intermediate financial or management accounts relating to the organization as a whole, or at least a fairly substantial part of it.

This may be a simple matter of listing the total figures produced by the payroll, debtors, creditors, and other feeder systems (computerized or manual) and entering them up once a month into a personal computer or ordinary bound ledger. More often in the public sector and any sizeable organization both the feeder system and the main accounting system are computerized and different balances are transferred at different periods from immediate on-line update, to weekly or annual transfers.

Figure 9.1 outlines a typical large main accounting system obtaining information from a number of feeder systems and producing trial balances,

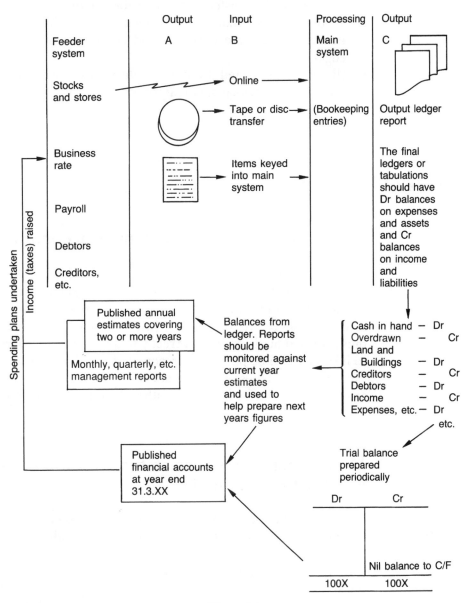

Figure 9.1

management accounts and estimates and year-end accounts. To answer the question raised above, the objectives of the system are usually to produce accurate, complete and valid accounts (in accordance with agreed or assumed answers to the more theoretical questions asked above) by ensuring:

1. all feeder account transactions (individually or bulk figures) are correctly and completely transferred to the main system;
2. all transactions transferred (including brought forward and carried forward figures) are correctly and completely updated to the relevant ledger account;
3. All figures extracted from the ledgers are correctly entered into the published or management accounts (balance sheet, revenue accounts, budgets, etc.).

Areas of key control

Reconciliations of feeder to main accounting systems

For all the feeder systems, manual or computerized, it is essential that line managers are able to ensure their data, i.e. instructions to the main system, are correctly and completely received and input to the main system, i.e. A to B in Figure 9.1. It is usually just as important to ensure that the input thus provided has been used correctly to update the appropriate accounts and so it should also be possible to reconcile from B to C or A to C. (The actual validity, completeness and accuracy of the output at A is usually taken to be an objective of the feeder system rather than the main accounting system.)

Monitoring of out-turn statements and preparation of management accounts

Nearly all public sector bodies are accountable to elected, political members or political appointees, though the link may, at times, be indirect as with health service boards or the accountability of individual state schools to local authority education committees or, ultimately, to an education minister. At the strategic political level the budget, its comparison to last year's approved spending and most importantly the implications for the next (possible election) year's spending is of prime importance. At times this focus on the relatively short-term spending and taxation requirements may seem shortsighted from a long-term planning viewpoint. Nevertheless detailed scrutiny of budgetary performance and future taxation focuses attention and demands political accountability in a way that is alien to most commercial accounts. Open political – and hence public – scrutiny generally acts to deter fraud and corruption. In most public bodies politicians will require verbal or written explanations of the main variations of out-turn expenditure against budgeted estimates at least once a year if not more frequently. Such explanation may well be reported in the press. Ideally, finance officers should monitor expenditure of various related budget headings and provide management with regular performance accounts and statistics as well as providing the political explanation.

These safeguards against fraud and corruption tend to operate to a greater or lesser extent in most public bodies, depending upon the accounting requirements of the body concerned. They are, or should be, first and foremost financial and management accounting controls hopefully ensuring adherence to policy objectives and good financial management. Nevertheless their importance in limiting fraud and corruption to a level generally recognized to be far lower than for private sector bodies should not be underestimated.

Control over output figures

Controls in this area have been discussed in Chapter 5. Most output is likely to be from computerized systems. It is important to maintain security of output not so much to avoid sensitive or personal data falling into the wrong hands, as is often the case with individual records, but to ensure that summarised totals and key performance data actually reach the relevant managers or other senior officials. A separation of input and output duties is often difficult if not impossible to maintain on a cost-effective basis. Also, any overspend or diversion of funds, while it may be possible to conceal on the micro-level by omitting particular line items from accounts will, on any serious scale, often show up as a variation on a budget head. Such a variation will require an explanation to senior management and quite likely politicians too, as described in the preceding section.

Bank reconciliation

This is no more than a particular reconciliation of the types already mentioned. However, it is of such fundamental importance as to warrant individual attention. In particular it is important to ensure that all bank accounts are reconciled. Most bodies will have separate accounts for income and expenditure and any balance should be transferred to an interest-bearing account at the end of the day's trading. Separate accounts may be kept for capital expenditure and investments and short-term borrowings depending upon the nature of the body. Any cash in transit or in the hands of officers (such as expenses imprests) should be verified on reconciliation.

Suspense accounts

All the ledger accounts merit attention and a set of ledgers kept to a high standard undoubtedly assists in deterring or revealing any fraud. But among all the accounts suspense accounts are particularly important and vulnerable. Any misappropriated shortages or gain that have to be held for a while will attract attention if transferred to a designated account and, even if they remain unnoticed for a short time, they will probably be picked up by a control account not balancing to zero at the end of the month or week. But a suspense account is often treated more favourably (from the fraudster's viewpoint). Most organizations will only clear out their suspense accounts once a year towards the year end. Until then unexplained balances of quite a genuine and innocent nature such as unexplained receipts or badly coded expenditure items will, for a time, help to conceal any fraudulent transaction. The specific circumstances under which suspense accounts can be used should be clearly set down and the movements into and out of suspense accounts should be independently authorized if control is to be effective.

Transfers and virement

So-called 'journal' transfers are largely a risk associated with local government, partly due to their year-end accounting procedures (see below) and partly due to their excessive proliferation of budget codes. Virement (the swapping of politically approved expenditure between budget headings) can take place in any public sector body. These procedures tend to add to the general complexity and reduce the open political accountability of the bodies' main accounts. Controls in this area may be lax if relatively junior officers, or a large number of senior officers, can with little need to explain or obtain independent authorization, transfer funds or budgets between coded headings. In this way monitoring (see above) and accountability can be seriously weakened. If lax control over transfers is combined with lax control over suspense accounts the combined risk may be even more serious.

Local authority accounts

Most public sector accounting differs from conventional accounting in the commercial sector. This is only to be expected. Once commercial motives such as the profit motive and motivations for maximizing the return on assets employed are forced to take second place to political motives the form of accounts and methods of reporting will require change. Sometimes this change is more subtle and hardly noticeable to the non-accountant, such as with the accounts of nationalized industries or direct service organizations. Sometimes the change is fundamental and very much the result of a separate evolution of accounting tradition. The accounts of local authorities, perhaps more than any other type of body, fall into this fundamentally different category. Most financial managers can come to terms with central government accounts with relative ease; the same might be said of health authorities, and this is becoming more so nowadays as these bodies adopt a more commercial style. Even though local authorities are also adopting a more commercial style of accounting some of the terms used may require additional explanation and this is provided to a basic level in Appendices 9.1 and 9.2.

Many readers will not be employed by local authorities. For this reason no further explanation or discussion beyond Appendices 9.1 or 9.2 is offered. As far as the aims of combating fraud and corruption are concerned a local authority is governed by the same considerations as other public bodies. Appendix 9.3 offers, for similar reasons, an explanation of some important terms peculiar to central government accounting.

Value for money, fraud and corruption

Good value for money and achieving a low risk of fraud and corruption are mutually supportive objectives. In the short term and on a small scale a situation might arise where an organization is forced to choose between the cost of internal control, say, employing extra staff in order to maintain separation of duties, and a saving on wages otherwise achieved. In the long run, if any organization is to be controlled by and accountable to its sponsors, their representatives, or service managers, it must have systems that are either self-checking – which implies adequate internal control – or that are sufficiently simple so as to be directly verifiable by senior management.

In the example of a choice between maintaining separation of duties and saving wages costs, senior management must be certain that the cost of wages saved is not being, or likely to be, offset by fraud. This implies they can demonstrate that all is well in respect to the transactions or values affected by the systems no longer subject to the separation of duties. For example, modern computerized payroll systems can often be operated by one or two officers whereas in the past many may have been required. A single officer might perhaps calculate and produce the payroll, and collect and disburse any cash wages. Clearly the scope for fraud is increased compared with a situation where each of these stages would probably involve separate officers with one effectively checking the work of another. To compensate for this lack of control, the management may need such additional controls as regular independent checks on the work of the payroll officer, or reviewing the overall level of payments on a regular basis taking account of fluctuations caused by pay rises, overtime requirements, etc. Sometimes computerization enables a natural separation between systems such as payroll and time recording to be utilized and the records to each to be reconciled in total.

Whatever the individual circumstances, the operation of the public sector organizations as a whole is utterly dependent upon an honest and largely fraud-free working environment if it is to offer anything approaching good value for money. The effective monopoly or near-monopoly situations of some bodies and the inevitable discretionary powers of most, mean that any corrupt management sooner or later (usually without any risk of bankrupting the body) can 'make a killing' no matter how they may appear at first to encourage competition, thrift and efficiency. It is always worth bearing in mind that for many public bodies the very compilation and dissemination of information used to provide measures of value for money are, to all intents and purposes, under the control of their management.

If value for money is to be bettered by adopting suitable competitive commercial methods the body concerned must be placed in a genuinely commercial environment and be able and expected to compete with similar organizations in a workable free-market situation. Several reported fraud cases and cases of serious mismanagement have highlighted examples of public sector bodies adopting the trappings of big business and a new commercial style of management when their underlying operational circumstances have remained largely unchanged. The ethos of open accountability had been shelved (temporarily at least) in favour of commercial confidence and achieving financial targets in what was still essentially a publicly funded near-monopoly situation. It may be argued that for a large public sector body, a transitional period is required while it adjusts to a market environment. If this is indeed the case then such a period should be particularly well controlled and monitored. For example, the accounts of many public sector bodies often display in great detail their spending and revenues sources (almost line item by line item in some cases). This may be useful to any political debate but it is in stark contrast to typical commercial accounts that seek to coalesce such detail into very few figures and provide the average reader with little that could seriously be considered to encourage accountability.

Much of the foregoing is subject to intense political debate and the author, without wishing to offend any particular viewpoint, seeks only to stress the importance of maintaining the openness and accountability of public sector bodies at a time of intense and often confusing changes in organizational structures and management attitudes.

Case study

Any case study produced in relation to this chapter would be likely to have more than the usual air of contrivance about it. Essentially, events causing fraud and corruption will almost inevitably relate less to the main accounting system than to the feeder systems that produce the accounting information and to which (including the political decision-makers and other outside parties) this information is distributed. Usually any fraud conceived by staff involved solely in the main accounting function will require collusion with others, though the case below examines a possible exception: the internal transfer of funds and falsification of related accounts.

Case study 9.1 The training and rehabilitation organization

The Training and Rehabilitation Organization (TRO) is sponsored by several government departments. It provides vocational skills and education to those who have been held for prolonged periods in institutions, such as prisons or mental hospitals, but are now considered fit for life in the general community. Approximately 50 approved training centres are in operation at any one time, in local colleges, schools (evenings), skill centres, etc. providing courses funded and approved by the TRO.

Each month income and expenditure statements are forwarded from each training centre to TRO headquarters, showing actual figures and progress against annual budget. Statements of student numbers are also sent at the start and end of each term.

At TRO HQ the income and expenditure (net) figures are input to the main accounting system to produce a subsidy total to draw against their 'grant-in-aid', a grant funded by central government. This is undertaken by the Chief Accountant at TRO HQ. Once the monthly subsidy figure has been calculated he fills this in on a return form to the relevant government department.

The chief accountant is also responsible for preparing the annual report and accounts of TRO and the monthly management reports. These are sent to the chief financial officer (CFO) and various line managers respectively. Occasionally the CFO requests various management accounts and the auditors (internal and external) may require copies of all sets of accounts on demand. The subsidy claim is also sent to the external auditors who may make a separate visit, independent of their audit of the annual accounts, to audit this claim. This is a short audit and basically involves agreeing the net total of each claim to the total of the subsidy. The auditor may also select about four or five of the claims for detailed checking and possibly undertake site visits to the approved training centres if any of the claim figures appear doubtful.

Throughout the year and particularly at the year end the chief accountant prepares 'journal transfers'. These are brief documents authorizing and recording the transfer of monies from one account to another. Transfers between accounts may, for example, be justified towards the year end if one is underspent and another would risk going over budget. This type of transfer is required to be approved by the CFO in order to avoid misrepresenting the validity of the initial budgets by virement between totally unrelated accounts. Another example is the requirement to correct errors and mispostings. This type of transfer is authorized entirely by the chief accountant, usually as a result of matters raised by one of his staff or one of the audit staff.

Given these procedures it was a relatively simple matter for the chief accountant to transfer funds between claims for training centres and the HQ budgets. Figure 9.2 suggests a possible method. This state of affairs might have continued indefinitely had not an internal audit value-for-money study involved a comparison of subsidy payments made to training centres to records of student numbers and noticed that very high payments appeared for several centres with very low student numbers. Further enquiries of the centres revealed the falsified claims held by the chief accountant.

Even in this example, systems outside the main accounting function have played a small part. This is almost inevitable if value is to be transferred to one of the staff involved in the accounts. Nevertheless Figure 9.2 illustrates the crucial controlling role of the chief accountant.

In this case the main accounting system failed because:

1. Journal transfers were not always countersigned, or at the very least made up by a junior accountant and authorized by the chief accountant.
2. There was a general lack of separation of duties involving the chief accountant. For example, the payments (or at least copy 1 of the claim) could have been sent directly to the training centres (and verification of the total sent to the chief accountant) from the government department.
3. The external auditor might have noticed the fraud if he had checked copy 3 of the claim (the accountant's copy made available to him during his visit) to copy 4, or copy 1 after this had been returned to

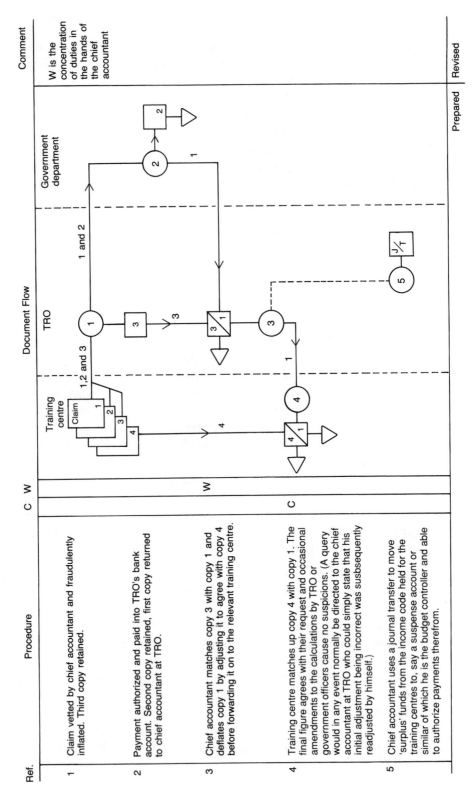

Training centre — TRO — Government department

W is the concentration of duties in the hands of the chief accountant

Ref.	Procedure	C	W
1	Claim vetted by chief accountant and fraudulently inflated. Third copy retained.		
2	Payment authorized and paid into TRO's bank account. Second copy retained, first copy returned to chief accountant at TRO.		W
3	Chief accountant matches copy 3 with copy 1 and deflates copy 1 by adjusting it to agree with copy 4 before forwarding it on to the relevant training centre.		
4	Training centre matches up copy 4 with copy 1. The final figure agrees with their request and occasional amendments to the calculations by TRO or government officers cause no suspicions. (A query would in any event normally be directed to the chief accountant at TRO who could simply state that his initial adjustment being incorrect was subsequently readjusted by himself.)	C	
5	Chief accountant uses a journal transfer to move 'surplus' funds from the income code held for the training centres to, say a suspense account or similar of which he is the budget controller and able to authorize payments therefrom.		

Prepared   Revised

Figure 9.2

the training centre. But very few visits were made to training centres and so the risk of detection was very low. The internal auditor had no effective right of access to the training centres and (as the money was repaid by central government) subsidy claims were considered low-priority internal audit work.
4. Routine audit attention given to suspense accounts was generally low as these were usually small in value in relation to the organization's income or expenditure, though not of course in relation to the chief accountant's personal income or expenditure.

Concluding points

This short chapter has singled out for particular attention an area of key control that applies to all financial and related systems where risks of fraud and corruption occur. As such it is a fitting final chapter of this book which has attempted to encompass a wide range of managerial and financial functions that occur in most organizations throughout the public sector. The main accounting system should act as the final safety net after all others have played their part. It is very rare for a fraud to be conceived and executed entirely within the accounting function if only because cash or value must flow to a third party for the fraud to occur. In the private sector the directors of a company may falsify the accounts to attract investments which they may squander in their own interest, or milk dry the reserves of the company. Even this will usually involve mechanisms within the feeder systems such as payments for dubious reasons to outside companies or additional unwarranted payments to directors. The mechanisms for senior public sector managers at director level to act in the same manner, though they exist, are usually present to a lesser degree.

It is vitally important for the public sector accountant never to lose sight of the purposes, especially the broadly political purposes, of the accounts. He or she should strive to maintain openness and accountability; to monitor and present the accounts in ways that best reveal the effects of policy and the performance of the management in meeting the policy objectives of the body.

The greater accountability of public sector accounts facilitates value for money. Achieving good value for money and low risk of fraud and corruption is, at least in the long run, a mutually supportive exercise.

Appendix 9.1 Accounting in local authorities

Accounts can be prepared on a cash basis, accruals basis or commitment basis for the organization as a whole or for individual funds (parts). Accounts can also be prepared on a budget basis or an actual basis. A combination of these is not unusual.

In local authorities both accruals-based and cash-based accounts are prepared on a fund basis, plus a consolidated balance sheet and funds flow statements, with budgeted and actual figures. Annual estimates are generally as important as the annual report and accounts and both are published.

The main types of published year-end accounts are, briefly, the following.

1. The general (or county) revenue account – the organization's main revenue account covering most areas of income and expenditure incurred throughout the financial year.
2. The general (consolidated) balance sheet – setting out the main balances as at the year end.
3. The housing revenue account – if a housing authority then the income and expenditure related to council housing must be shown in a separate account.
4. Direct service organizations (DSO) accounts – separate balance sheets, revenue accounts and notes must be made up for each DSO.
5. The collection fund account – this is a separate revenue account required by law to show the income and costs incurred in collecting the community charge and business rates.

Any other funds held under separate legal requirements such as pension funds are also normally shown as separate fund accounts.

In addition to these published accounts internal trading accounts are likely to be required under the terms of the government's recent green paper *Competing for Quality*, November 1991.

The interested reader is recommended to obtain (usually free of charge) a set of his or her local authority's accounts. The accounting requirements are subject to considerable change at present.

Appendix 9.2 Terms used in local authority accounting

Debt charges In local authorities both the capital repayment and interest element of the debt charge are charged to the revenue accounts as opposed to the interest-only element in most commercial accounts.

Deferred capital receipts (Cr) (Usually on financing side of the balance sheet) Usually capital receipts (income) are owed to the council on sold property.

This is needed to show deferred income to balance loans deferred (see below). For example, when a council house is sold and a council mortgage is granted, money is received as the council mortgage is paid off. In the meantime a deferred charge is set up to show debt owed to the council (Dr) which will be balanced against either a deferred capital receipt (Cr) or a loan still owed by the council on the property sold (Cr) or parts of both.

Deferred charges (Dr) (Usually placed with long-term debtors on Balance Sheet) Capital payments for which no fixed asset is held; they are set up to balance Cr entry for, say, capital grants or long-term debts owed from mortgages and other long-term loans outstanding on properties sold.

Capital discharged The payments made to date to pay off the debt on the capital assets or other long-term outlay (OLTO) show on the balance sheet. (Capital assets are usually shown on the balance sheet at historic cost, often the cost of the debt or estimated proportion thereof used to finance the asset, unlike in commercial accounting where the market value of the asset is shown. This practice is subject to increasing erosion as more and more assets are revalued.)

Capital employed All assets used. This is sometimes, confusingly, taken as gross assets (fixed and current) but usually current assets are netted off against current liabilities. Some public bodies are required by law to make a laid-down percentage return on their capital employed. See Rate of return below.

Capital programme The capital projects to be undertaken over one or, sometimes, up to five years. Capital programmes are financed by borrowing, RCCO or capital receipts.

1. RCCO: revenue contributions to capital outlay. Usually taken from the general fund to finance building programmes.
2. Capital receipts applied/unapplied (spent/unspent): unlike companies, local authorities are subject to very many legal restrictions upon what type and how much of a capital receipt can actually be spent and on what it can be spent.

Consolidated loans fund (CLF) Loans are raised to meet the borrowing requirements of a whole authority, usually on quite advantageous terms, from sources such as the Public Works Loans Board or major City institutions. These funds are managed by the CLF through which internal advances are made to the spending committees at a smoothed, i.e. constant, interest rate and internal repayments made which, over the long term, meet the cost of external borrowings. Thus each spending committee benefits from predictable and lower interest charges and lower administrative costs. Not all authorities use a CLF.

Funds/reserves These are accumulations of income. In future the term 'funds' will probably fall into disuse as the law now requires 'provisions' for specific foreseeable uses and 'reserves' for other capitalized accumulations of income. The term 'fund' may still be used in a wider sense to describe the housing fund, general fund, collection fund, etc. as a way of distinguishing the different purposes of the main categories of accounts.

Rate of return A statutory percentage of capital employed, e.g. profits as a percentage of capital employed (usually calculated on a current cost basis).

(For more detailed explanations see the *Local Authority Accounts Glossary* published by CIPFA.)

Appendix 9.3 Terms used in central government accounting

Central government accounts appear, gradually, to be moving towards a more commercial style compared to the simplistic, but very understandable, receipts and payments accounts. Much of the terminology is, however, still distinctive. Indeed it is difficult to talk about accounting arrangements of this or that department without involving almost macro-economic terms.

Accounting officer: usually the permanent head of a ministry or department. He or she will be held directly responsible at a political level for the accounts and much else. Accounting officers are rarely qualified accountants.

Appropriation accounts: These are much more all embracing than the appropriation part of a set of, say, manufacturing accounts. They are the year-end accounts of a government body or major spending programme, outlining how the monies voted have been spent and accounting for any surplus or deficit. Additional accruals-based statements of assets and liabilities may be given.

Appropriations in aid: income received by departments which they are allowed, with treasury approval, to retain. This income can then be utilized directly whereas the usual procedure is to surrender receipts to the Consolidated fund (see below).

Comptroller and Auditor General (C&AG): head of the National Audit Office (NAO) and also responsible for the issue of payments from the exchequer (from accounts held at the Bank of England). The C&AG reports on the audit of government bodies, undertaken by the NAO, to the Public Accounts Committee of parliament.

Consolidated fund: a central fund for most government income, operated on behalf of all departments and most subsidiary bodies.

Estimates: as the name suggests, an annual budget for each main spending programme. They are presented to parliament and voted upon, after which they are termed 'votes' and compared to expenditure in the appropriation accounts.

National Loans Fund: a fund for controlling all borrowings of government and lending therefrom mostly to public sector bodies.

Public expenditure borrowing requirement (PSBR): net expenditure after taxation and other income, required to be funded by government borrowing, on behalf of central, local, and related government bodies.

Virement: official treasury sanction of the transfer of voted funds between various approved 'subheads' of expenditure in the votes.

Further reading

The following is an arbitrary selection of further information the author has found interesting or useful.

Fraud and corruption

Auditing Practices Board 'Audit Guidelines in relation to Fraud, other irregularity and errors', *Auditing and Reporting*, CCAB, UK.

Audit Commission for Local and Health Authorities in England and Wales (1981, 1984, 1987, 1990). *Surveys of Computer Fraud*.

Albrecht, S. W. *Determining Fraud. The Internal Auditor's Perspective*. IIA (USA).

Bologna, G. J. and Lindquist, R. J. (1984). *Fraud Auditing and Forensic Accounting*. Wiley, New York.

CIPFA (1989). *The Investigation of Fraud in the Public Sector*. CIPFA *Financial Information Service* Vol 3 pt 3.1.6. Collier, P. A., Dixon, R. and Marston, C. L. *The Prevention and Detection* (1990) *of Computer Fraud* IIA and CIMA, London.

Comer, M. J. *Corporate Fraud*. McGraw Hill

Doig, A., *Corruption and Misconduct in Contemporary British Politics*.

Elliot, R. K. and Willingham, J. J. '*Management Fraud Detection and Deterrence*'. PCI Books.

ICAEW (1987) *Countering Computer Fraud*.

Levi, M. *The Prevention of Fraud* Home Office, Crime Prevention Unit.

Office of Fair Trading (1976) *Cartels, Detection and Remedies – A Guide for Local Authorities.*

Parker, B. D. (1976). *Crime by Computer* Charles Scriber, New York.

Russell, H. *Foozles and Frauds*, IIA (USA).

Vinten, G. (ed.) (1990) 'Focus on Fraud', *Managerial Auditing Journal*, Vol. 5. No. 4.

Capital projects and major contracts Chapter 4

CIPFA (1989) *A Guide to Financial Management and Audit of contracts.* Chartered Institute of Public Finance and Accountancy, London.

CIPFA (1983) *Contract Audit Guidance Notes* Chartered Institute of Public Finance and Accountancy, London.

CIPFA (1984) *Contract Audit (Site visit) Guidance Notes*, Chartered Institute of Public Finance and Accountancy, London.

Chappel, D. (1987) *Understanding JCT Standard Building Contracts*, International Thompson.

CIPFA (1984) *A Management Guide to Contracting Out Services in Local Government*, Chartered Institute of Public Finance and Accountancy, London.

General audit and accounting and Chapters 3 and 9

Audit Commission for Local and Health Authorities in England and Wales (1988). *Code of Local Government Audit Practice for England and Wales.* CIPFA (1987) *Computer Audit Guidelines.*

CIPFA (1991) *Code of Practice on Local Authority Accounting in Great Britain* (including 'Guidance Notes for Practitioners').

Fletcher C. G. M. (1991) *Government Accounting* ICAS.

HMSO *Government Accounting.*

Jones, P. and Bates, J. (1990). *Public Sector Auditing* Chapman & Hall, London.

Jones R. and Pendlebury M. *Public Sector Accounting* Pitman.

Means tested benefits, Chapter 8

CIPFA (1987) *Housing Benefit Audit – A good practice guide.* CIPFA, London.

Ward, M. and Zebedee, J. *Guide to Housing Benefit and Community Charge Benefit*, SHAC and Institute of Housing, London.

Index